MEXICAN HOMES OF TODAY

MEXICAN
HOMES of TODAY

By Verna Cook Shipway and Warren Shipway

ARCHITECTURAL BOOK PUBLISHING CO., INC.

NEW YORK

Frontispiece "EL PÁRAJO"

A dramatic concept in the form of a colossal bird by sculptor Mathias Goeritz marks the entrance to Jardines del Bosque in Guadalajara.

Photograph by Horst Hartung

Title Photo

An indelible and profound Indian tradition continues to lie beneath the surging influences upon Mexico. Of pre-Conquest Zapotec culture is this wondrous ceramic figure of their Corn God.

Photograph by Guillermo Zamora

Published simultaneously in Canada
by S. J. Reginald Saunders, Publishers, Toronto 2B.

Library of Congress Catalog Card Number: 64-8118

Printed in the United States of America

CONTENTS

V

Contents

VI

FOREWORD

In its vigorous advance, Mexican architecture is viewed as producing works of quality and of strong plastic interest by the forthright and far-seeing publication, *Arquitectura*. Its character, now rich in depth and in future, was originally formed by the logical blending of two kindred currents, the French of Le Corbusier with the German of Bauhaus — Gropius, Mies van der Rohe and Neutra. To this, Mexico has added an unique enrichment, continues the editorial, a "fundamental fusing of the principles of modern architecture with those of its past."

This fusion is a merger of simplified forms with the needs of today's Mexican living, all in bond with the country's traditions. These traditions are more than hearsay; they are inherent in its people. They are neither solely of the mind, nor of the blood. Actually one walks on their underlying strata; evidences of centuries past continue to be found underfoot. And so, instinctively and with faith in her talents, the architecture of Mexico, like her murals, has strength, sincerity and pronounced individuality.

The aim of these pages is to show the approach and strides into the future of the Mexican home. It is by no means a technical survey of cause and effect, but the impressions of a creative abundance received by us and our camera. We are hopeful that these photographic sallies will convey a warm and vital picture of this many faceted subject.

And so it happens that in a country which today is far from being homogenized, there is a lack of uniformity in its contemporary domestic architecture. Change of design with its differing adaptations and versions is apt to become enmeshed in local custom, reflecting regional artifacts and color preferences. In designing Mexicans become bored, as do the Chinese, with copying. To them it is far more enjoyable, in fact easier, to think of something new.

The assembly of this material was a pleasurable experience; amusing at times, frequently unique and invariably interesting. It was our very good fortune to receive sympathetic aid on every hand. We offer our appreciation to the staff of Arno Brehme for the manner in which they handled our photographic efforts. And to those who extended their hospitality, so typical of Mexico, we will be continually indebted.

PICTURE LOCATIONS

*Below, Spanish names of owners are listed alphabetically by surname or father's name.
Where a following surname is used, it is the family name of the owner's mother.*

X

XI

Picture Locations

XIV

XV

GLOSSARY

Italicized Spanish words appearing in the captions are defined below

AGUADOR.................. stand for water jugs

AHUEHUETE.................. an ancient sabine tree

ALBERCA.................. pool

ANDAS.................. portable platform for carrying Santo

ÁNIMA.................. soul, spirit

AZOTEA.................. flat roof

AZULEJO.................. glazed tile

BALCÓN.................. balcony

BALCÓN CORRIDO.................. running balcony

BANDERA.................. banner, flag; a Mexican plant

BARANDAL.................. banister or railing

BAROQUE.................. term used today for art style, period 1600 to 1720. Originally from "barroco," meaning irregularly shaped pearl and used to describe the ornate or bizarre. An outgrowth of Renaissance, originating in Rome. After its transplanting by the Spanish to their American Colonial empire, the Baroque became a true architectural style of the New World.

BATEA.................. tray, bowl

BRASERO.................. a charcoal stove, a brazier, a fire-pan

Glossary

BUTACA .... armchair, easy chair

CABALLERO .... gentleman, horseman

CALLE .... street

CANAL, CANALES .... projecting roof drains, eaves trough

CANCELA .... screening door from zaguán to patio

CANTERA .... quarry stone, stone block

CAOBA .... mahogany

CAPIALZADO .... arched treatment over some doors and windows for purpose of spreading and increasing light.

CHURRIGUERESQUE .... a peculiarly Spanish outcome of the Baroque
style; the utmost in architectural unrestraint, and wondrous intricacy.
Named after José Churriguera, Spanish architect (about 1660-1725).

CINCELADO .... minute carving principally upon estofado

CITARILLA .... open fence or balustrade usually built of shaped brick or
tile

COMEDOR .... dining room

CONCHA .... shell; shell ornament

CORREDOR .... gallery around a patio

CRISTO .... Christ; image of Christ crucified

CRUZ DE ÁNIMAS .... Cross of the Souls, completely Mexican, depicting
Crucifixion with souls in Purgatory

ESTANCIA .... sitting room, living room

ESTÍPITE .... pilaster in the form of inverted pyramid, characteristically
        Churrigueresque

ESTOFADO .... painting on a gilt ground

GESSO .... coating of Plaster of Paris or gypsum for use in painting

HACIENDA .... estate, large farm; income producing property

JARDINES del PEDREGAL .... Residential section carved from lava fields
        in the southerly part of Mexico City

LLAMADOR .... door knocker

LOS OCHO CABALLOS .... the eight horses

MAGUEY .... the century plant

MANIERISTA .... style period between Baroque and the Renaissance

MEDIO-PAÑO .... one-half handkerchief, a contraction of MEDIO-
        PAÑUELO

MILAGROS .... votive offerings, silver "thank" symbols

MIRADOR .... penthouse, enclosed balcony commanding an extensive view

MONJA .... nun

PALAPA .... leaf of tree palm used for thatching

PÁRAJO .... bird

PILA .... stone trough, basin

PILÓN, PILONES .... basin; mortar for grinding grain or as used in sugar refining

PINO .... pine

PINO de CHIHUAHUA .... pine from Chihuahua

PLATERESQUE .... Plateresco period in Spain from 16th to first-half of 17th century. Finely scaled decoration derives its name from "plateros" or silversmiths' art.

POSTIGO .... small opening or panel in a door of larger size

QUIOSCO .... kiosk, pavillion, summer house

RAMADA .... arbor, covered shed

REBOSO .... long, straight scarf used as a shawl by Mexican women

RECÁMARA .... dressing room; bedroom

REJA .... grating; railing

ROCOCO .... era between death of Louis XIV in 1715 and execution of Louis XVI in 1793. Charming and extravagant in design, often referred to as the last of the universal styles.

SABINO .... water cypress of Mexico "Arbol de la Noche Triste"

SALA .... formal room, parlor

SALA GRANDE .... hall, large parlor

SANTOS .... images of Saints, both Santos (m.) and Santas (f.)

SOMBRERO .... hat
TABLERO .... panel
TALAVERA .... glazed pottery made from beginning of 16th century under
        Spanish domination, now continuing in more Mexican character.
TERRAZA .... terrace; open gallery.
TEZONTLE .... porous building-stone from volcanic rock
ZAGUÁN .... open passageway through house to patio
ZAPATA .... corbel, short timber placed lengthwise under girder at top of
        post, post cap
ZONPANTLI .... native Indian tree of Mexico

The Archangel Gabriel, impressive in size, with his right arm raised in a gesture of salutation welcomes the reader. The flesh tones of his face, arms and legs have deepened with age until they blend with the gilded robes and with the gold which picks out the tips of his dull-green feathered wings.

Home of Althea Revere

Deep red bougainvillaea, billowing over the green and pink *cantera* arches, forms
a luxuriant base for the elegance of the yellowish-pink stucco façade above.

1

Behind the arches of the guest wing on the preceding page, this arcade runs the full length of the entrance courtyard. Leading from it to the rooms immediately above, is the sculptural flight of steps in the foreground. Treads, some on a solid base and the remainder cantilevered from the house wall, circle an old *zapote* tree which rises above the terrace connecting the wing with the main house.

The color harmony of materials used with recurring greens of potted planting, gives added charm to the delightful calm of this old-world area. Salmon-colored brick forming the shallow barrel vaults, blend with the burned clay flooring tile, and again, with the pink stucco of the spiral stair base. Beyond the stairs, but only partially visible here, the interior wall is haphazardly splashed with flirting orchids, adding gaiety to the severity of the masonry.

Home of Althea Revere

unpatterned severity
and great elegance

form the entrance to a house built for himself in the environs of Mexico City by architect, Juan Sordo Madaleno. On a stark, white masonry wall some twenty feet high, hangs this commanding figure, a sorrowful Christ, formed with three heavy bars of wrought iron. Here, Mathias Goeritz, sculptor, has used with utmost simplicity a basic material without ostentation, to portray a timeless event. It is the focal point of the courtyard, whose austere walls are relieved, here and there, by grouped planting and the brilliance of geraniums.

5

Part of an unusual entrance hall to an unusual home. Yellowed light through a plastic roof is filtered by muslin on the soft canary walls. Paper flowers in yellow and magenta carry the eye to a handprinted silkscreen copy of an ancient horse, in grays, black, and yellows from Lascaux Cave.

Except for a small wooden crucifix from 9th century Spain, unadorned off-white walls rise from a high-piled golden carpet, in contrast with the effective veining of the *sabino* furniture wood. Startling in bougainvillaea red, the hand-loomed cover of the low table is complemented by a casual row of pillows in violent pink, purple, yellow and again, bougainvillaea red.

7

Echoing the austerity of an old Spanish interior while advancing hand-in-hand with the contemporary, this lower hall in white and gold leads to the swimming pool and gardens.

8

A silver figure of La Virgen del Camino, patroness of travelers, provides a note of gorgeousness. Above and behind her crown a triple layered nimbus, with delicate rays of silver, then gold, against a background of pleated silver, sparkles with crystals. Her enameled face bears an expression of serenity as she holds the Christ Child in one hand and in the other, a crystal globe. To complete this exquisite statuette, a conical shaped robe, embossed and studded with simulated rubies, diamonds, and emeralds rises above a half moon, a pair of wheels, and a swirl of cherubs.

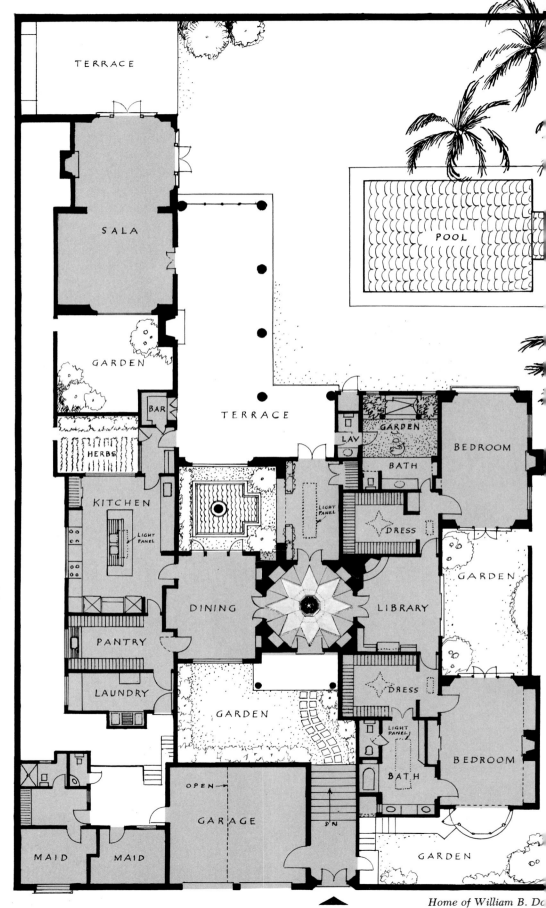

light

inner

gardens

and

murmuring

waters

TERRACE

SALA

GARDEN

BAR

TERRACE

HERBS

KITCHEN

Light Panel

DINING

PANTRY

LIBRARY

LAUNDRY

GARDEN

MAID

MAID

OPEN

GARAGE

DN

POOL

GARDEN

LAV

BATH

BEDROOM

LIGHT PANEL

DRESS

GARDEN

DRESS

LIGHT PANEL

BATH

BEDROOM

GARDEN

Home of William B. Do

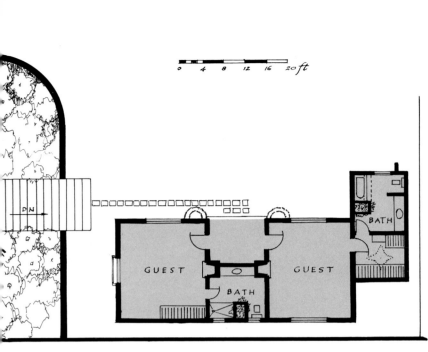

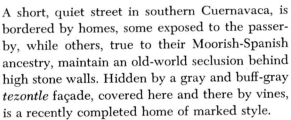

A short, quiet street in southern Cuernavaca, is bordered by homes, some exposed to the passer-by, while others, true to their Moorish-Spanish ancestry, maintain an old-world seclusion behind high stone walls. Hidden by a gray and buff-gray *tezontle* façade, covered here and there by vines, is a recently completed home of marked style.

The property is L-shaped, running from street to street, with the natural grades sloping east and south. Although surrounded on all but the north by other homes, complete apartness is made possible by the use of retaining and garden walls above grade, all without obstructing the awe-inspiring, easterly view of snow-capped Popo-catepetl and Iztaccihuatl.

Even a brief study of the plan will show how well it lends itself to both entertaining and every-day living. Circulation, to and from the service areas equipped with all kinds of modern conveniences, is excellent for easy housekeeping. And the various rooms, already generous in size, by opening upon planted inner courts or the main sweep of lawn, are given an added feeling of spaciousness.

An unusual feature, not shown in these pictures, is the generous use of opaque-glass ceiling panels to filter the sunlight over otherwise dark interior spaces.

The octagonal foyer with walls painted a subtle light gray has a pyramidal ceiling terminating in amber glass. In the center of the gray *cantera* stone floor, the greater part of which is stained brown and outlined with tile to form a star, is a small fountain. Here, a brass sprite dances in little jets of water, which, filling the flower-scattered basin, falls with a whisper into the glass-and-wrought-iron curbed pool below.

Four niches with carved stone urns and their vigorous planting, give an added air of elegance. Intermediate openings are trimmed in gray *cantera* and outlined by 3½ inch painted bands of pale pink. In the background on the facing page is shown the interior of the main entrance doors leading to the street.

This magnificent *cancela* between *terraza* and *sala*, is from the now demolished home in Morelia of Agustín de Iturbide, hailed in 1821 as "Libertador" and who, for some eight months later, was Agustín I, Emperador of Mexico.

The carved medallions in the circular heading, the transom and the side panels, are repeated in wood and stone throughout the house to become a leitmotif in the rhythm of the decorations.

Immediately to the left of the foyer is the beamed dining room, with its wide expanse of glass on each side framing the greenery of the entrance and fountain courts. The ceiling areas between the beams, sideboard recess and the forcefully modeled shell above are gray as the foyer walls, while the remaining surfaces are gray with a greenish caste. A deep-piled, light gray rug covers the hexagonal brick floor.

In the moderate climate of Cuernavaca, this delightful *terraza* overlooking the *alberca* and open to the south, while its other three sides give protection from capricious breezes, is a center for casual living. Although it also serves as the covered connection between the *sala* and the other rooms, there is because of its generous proportions, no feeling of constriction. Here the heavily beamed roof is carried by the soft green house wall and the massive light gray *cantera* columns at the garden side. The two major furniture groupings, one at the fireplace in the foreground and the other at the far end, are placed on lacelike sisal matting from Pátzcuaro. The pale pink of the painted iron furniture blends with the soft rose and yellow of the woven fabric covering the tufted cushions, which in turn repeats the color of the matting.

16

Two views of the *sala*, a room of today although from positive Colonial antecedents. A highly waxed brick floor is substantially covered with two heavy greyish-green rugs, repeating the color of the walls. The several sofas and chairs are upholstered in soft shades of blue-green, celadon, green stripes on pinkish white and salmon pinks, giving grace and verve to a tender color scheme.

Against a lustrous tiled wall, tropical planting at each end of the sunken tub forms backgrounds for the carved, white *cantera* lintel and its two supporting columns. The seven foot strip of grass (when asked by the designer if he would like to have a grass floor in part of his bathroom, Mr. Dolph blandly replied, "Why certainly, what other type of flooring could one possibly have?") is crossed on stepping stones of sea motifs to the recessed fixtures along the near wall. An interior area, but flooded with light through its conservatory ceiling of glass.

19

The sun terrace at the east wall of the *sala* is partially illuminated at night by these two distinctive, finely pierced brass lanterns on their wrought iron scrolls. The light adobe-tan wall is capped by a cornice of three tiers of red half-tile, their open ends filled with white cement.

Below is the inviting covered entry to the guest house at the south end of the garden.

Set into the robust and continuous masonry walls which border the principal *calle* of San Miguel de Allende, is this merry pair of doors, undeniably French in arrangement of paneling and in the spontaneity of design.

Native carving of wood was a fine art in pre-Conquest days. Later, because of the heavy demands by the Spanish for more and more works in wood, both massive and elaborate, it became, for the most part, a craft.

22

A brass sunburst 10″ long

Gold leaf originally covered these two panels but only a glimmer remains. In their exuberance, they clearly reflect the inherited art of the craftsmen.

23

With Louis XV spirit, free-flowing curves, gold-leafed against a background of blue, frolic casually around this important frame of wood, over four feet high.

A group of unusual frames from Peru with Mexican kinship. Small paintings on wood portraying Santiago, Mary "Queen of the World," and an unknown Madonna are surrounded by extravagantly carved wood, gessoed and then gold leafed. This lavishness is accentuated by sparkling mirror facets. Each frame measures about 24 inches in height. These treasures are now being reproduced in Mexico with the substitution of mirrors for the central paintings.

25

La Parroquia de Santiago, Marfil, Gto.

"*Baroque*, word of distain and depreciation, word of enchantment and artistic significance! The world movement of the *Baroque*, to which such giants as Rembrandt and Bach belonged and which ended in the fluffy *Rococo* of Europe and the bewildering Mexican *Churrigueresque* in America, has been for 200 years the background of artistic development in the Spanish-American Colonies. Already in the 16th century the Indians embraced most eagerly and cleverly new ideas brought over from Europe; but perhaps to no other stylistic impulse did they take more vigorously and whole heartedly than to the *Baroque*." Baron Alexander von Wuthenau

26

From a deserted chapel near San Miguel de Allende, this carved stone frame together with its plank doors was brought over the mountains by burros to Marfil. The frame was given importance by raising its cornice and inserting other stones, some with little weatherworn figures in high relief, to form an overdoor treatment. The final result is one of unusual naïveté and quaintness.

27

Here are two views of a room that cherishes the calm and serenity of the past while living interestingly in the present. A truly cheerful room, generously supplied with light from a wide inner court and through the circular-headed windows overlooking gardens to the south.

On a magnificently carved and formerly gold-leafed cross, 47 inches high, is nailed a *Cristo,* with His crown of thorns, in gilded silver.

Home of Mrs. Gordon Hicks

29

A bird cage fantasy in wire trimmed with brass edgings, galleries and insertions. Revolving perches sway back and forth and completely around in its elaborately arched loft.

Home of Althea Revere

A high ceilinged *sala* and dining area of distinguished proportions. Here, recurring motifs in gold leaf over a base of bole start immediately above the stained and polished brown floor-brick with the richly carved apron of a former *andas*, now adapted for use as a coffee table. Then, repeated in the mouldings of the wood mantel, its frieze and extravagant columns, they terminate in the intricate piercings of the magnificent mirror frame, high on the white wall.

(*Left*) Hand-hewn framing members, supported by heavy girders, carry the ceiling brick. A painted white triangle on each brick contrasts with the natural burned-clay color.

31

two ranking artists

Dorcas & Oliver Snyder

restore

an old house in

San Miguel de Allende

Beyond a pair of imposing and dignified old urns, richly carved from chocolate *cantera*, nestles a *quiosco* in the angle formed by two high garden walls. A hint of the Orient, so congenial with Mexican tastes, runs up the lacelike supports of wrought iron and centers in a hanging lantern fashioned of expanded metal lath. A typically indigenous note is the use of burro pads for outdoor seats and cushions.

From this *quiosco*, across the patio, above white oleanders and over soft-red roof eaves, rises in the distance, the great dome of Monjas de la Concepción. Its inspiration, so it is said, came from the vast cupola of the Hôtel des Invalides in Paris.

(Opposite page)

Over a niche-shell with softly curving ribs and flutes, hangs a high-held swag made of an unusual hand-loomed hammock from Guadalajara. The eight-branched chandelier is painted a grayed ochre to contrast with ceiling brick and walls of white. The floor tile is white, inset with a star pattern in dull ochre. Wooden ceiling beams have been scraped to a weathered gray.

This 350-year-old house was converted into a gracious and graceful home by its owners. Since the relatively low glazed doors, which ill accorded with the 15 foot ceiling height, were in a street wall, San Miguel de Allende's custom permitted no change in the size of the opening. Cleverly, the niche head gave added height over these doors and to create a still more pronounced up-lift, the swag was added to extend the entire composition to beam height.

Sala de Artes

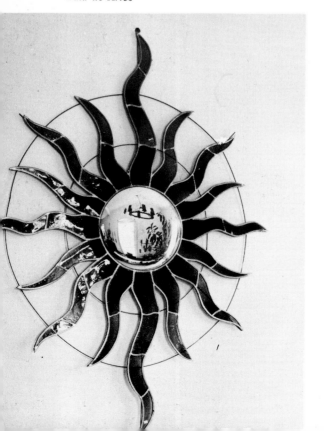

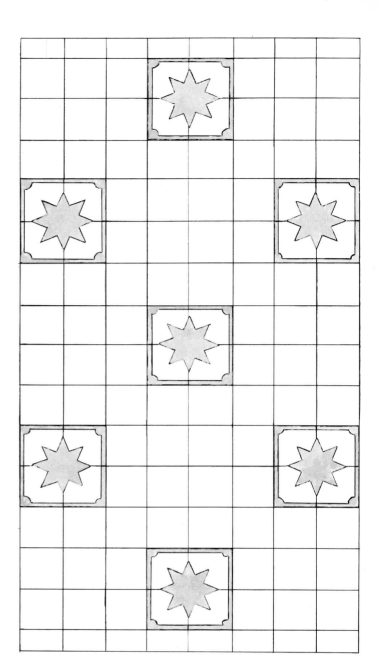

floor tile

0   1   2   3 ft

From a brilliant convex center mirror, amber rays of handmade, wavy glass set in lead cames, flame out to an overall length of 53 inches and a width of 40 inches.

Home of Norman Mac Gregor Jr.

One wonders at the use of tin for exterior lanterns but, like many "can't-be-dones," this metal, when given a reasonable amount of care such as an occasional thin coat of linseed oil, has lasted for decades without serious deterioration. The captivating caprice above sits on a garden wall, housing a wandering snail. Each of its hexagonal sides is topped with a glazed triangle containing a metal rosette.

Airy, fanciful and shimmering with gold spray, this chandelier of French concept was crafted in San Miguel de Allende, a town noted for its work in tin.

Home of Dorcas & Oliver Snyder

The pierced, shell-like cresting and flare at base give distinction to a lantern of tin from Morelia, with alternating clear and rippled amber lights.

Here copper was used to fabricate this fixture of more complicated design (*lower left*).

Another copper lantern, octagonal in form, with a lush crown and base, lends elegance to a kitchen (*lower right*).

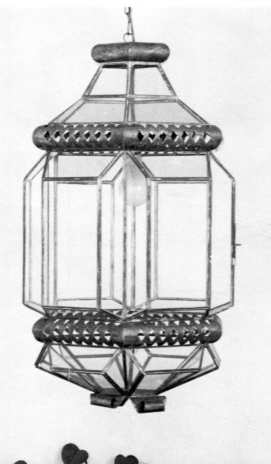

around an atrium

Opposite, a pair of massive old doors, in part reconstructed. Above a small tin of fresh flowers, a panel carries the first three letters of IHSUS, or Jesus, in Greek, while on the other half, above a bronze *llamador* of possible Venetian origin, a panel bears the monogram of the Virgin Mary.

The doors open, and for the moment, you wonder if you are not viewing the atrium of an ancient Roman home with its surrounding peristyle.

Home of Hans-Joachim von Block

A study of the plan on page 43 is necessary in order to appreciate the many advantages of this unusual home, a possible modern forerunner of the current trend.

Upon entering, you are at once conscious of a feeling of ease and amplitude, enhanced by an impressive repetition of the light-green *cantera* columns. This feeling builds up as you pass the open court with its murmuring fountain.

Here, from the easterly side of the three-walled *estancia* bordering the peristyle, is a view of the interior spaciousness on which open the many rooms around its perimeter. Colors are restrained but far from negative; the beams spanning the columns and the fireplace wall are painted in what is known as Mexican pink, a baffling and enchanting color. Unpainted brick riding on dark stained-wood joists form the ceilings and above the highly waxed, brown floor tile, rise walls of peach-white.

A view into the old basin of green Oaxaca *cantera,* with its eight acanthus buttresses.

The fountain has functional as well as decorative values. With the high pressure available and an adjustable head, the flow of water can be practically atomized. Thus, on an uncomfortably hot, dry day, it is possible, by merely turning a valve, to produce an atmosphere of delightful coolness in the surrounding areas. The stone paving of the atrium is exceptionally handsome. Alternating with 17-inch-square slabs of gray lava rock are slightly cushioned panels in the "Margaritas" pattern. Eight narrow strips radiate from a large crowned pebble, all of yellow fieldstone, while the intervening spaces are filled with thin lava spalls.

The open side of the *estancia* with its generous fireplace. Doors to the left give access to a raised terrace and to the swimming pool in the garden below.

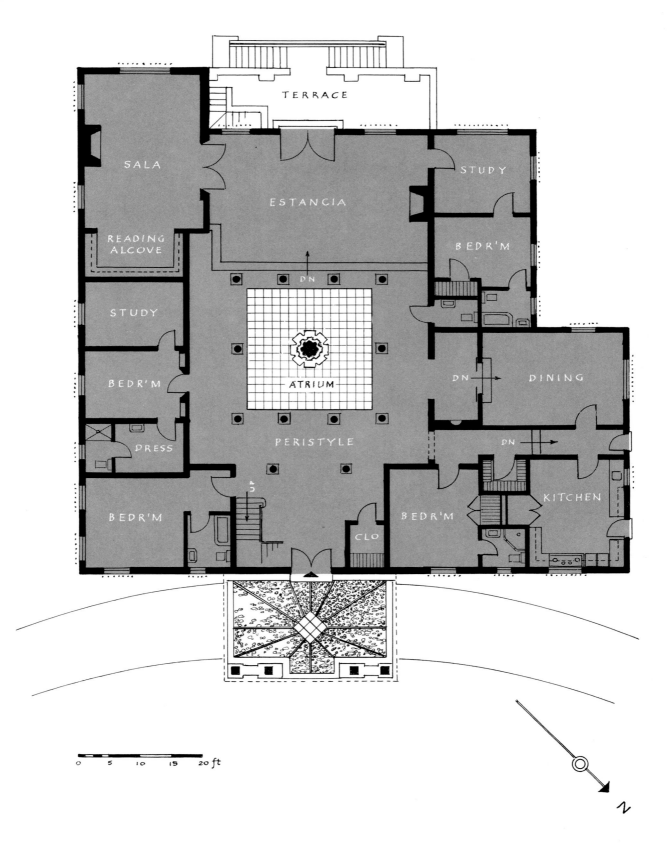

TERRACE

SALA

ESTANCIA

STUDY

READING ALCOVE

BEDR'M

STUDY

DN

BEDR'M

ATRIUM

DN

DINING

DRESS

PERISTYLE

DN

BEDR'M

KITCHEN

UP

CLO

BEDR'M

0   5   10   15   20 ft

N

Upon leaving the von Block home, you overlook an interestingly patterned paving in the form of a geometric sunburst under the carriage porch. Beyond, a masonry retaining wall outlined in scallops carries the carved stone *pila* of another fountain.

A small, white marble dolphin from Rome spouts a thin stream of water, which falls over the edges of the upper basin into the half-quatrefoil-shaped pool.

Carápan

Carved from hard pink *cantera*, the Archangel San Rafael stands with a fish in one hand and a torch in the other, against a blue wall. The original shell-like base which seemed too small for the figure, now serves as a pseudo halo. This representation of the guardian angel of all humanity is said to have been removed from the atrium of a small church near Querétaro.

45

A wool rooster in blacks, reds, whites and tweed-grays against a rich yellow background, 33 x 36 inches, stands ready to announce the coming day — his eye fixed on the fading morning star while the sun rises in the lower right hand corner.

On this, the facing page and the page following are examples of the highly original tapestries designed and loomed by Saul Borisov, a gifted artist. Using a variety of colors, different kinds of threads, and divers weaving techniques, the effects achieved are sometimes exciting, sometimes calm, but always arresting.

This tired, spotted bull with dangling tongue, is of black and white wool except for his horns and some light spots which are woven with *maguey* thread to give added sheen. Behind him, a matador in black holds a cape in two shades of red, with the surrounding background a more brilliant red. This striking work is 36 x 52 inches.

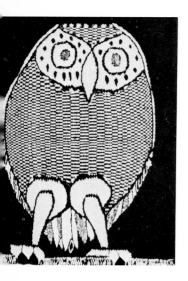

Some of Borisov's calmer conceptions.

On the left, a pensive owl has body feathers expertly woven in perspective of white cotton outlined with brown. Face and legs are of cream colored *maguey* fiber while the background is woven from dark brown wool.

Rising from an old-gold vase on an off-white ground are flowers in deep red, dark blue and lavender. Their green leaves shade into brown with stems nearing black. All loomed in wool except the centers of the flowers, which are embroidered.

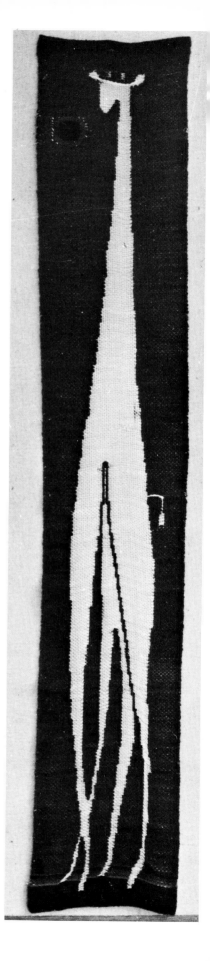

A truly magnificent giraffe, 70 inches high, done in a white cotton open-net weave, with a golden-yellow wool background.

The "Scarlotti" is one of the designs of Cynthia Sargent Riggs in whose workshop these deep piled, luxurious rugs are produced. Measuring 8 x 12 feet, a nosegay of colors — fuchsia, reds, gold, dark purple, green, pink, mustard and soft shades of blue — form a novel pattern on a white field. Through the dying, spinning and hooking, all the work is done by hand under Mrs. Riggs' supervision.

49

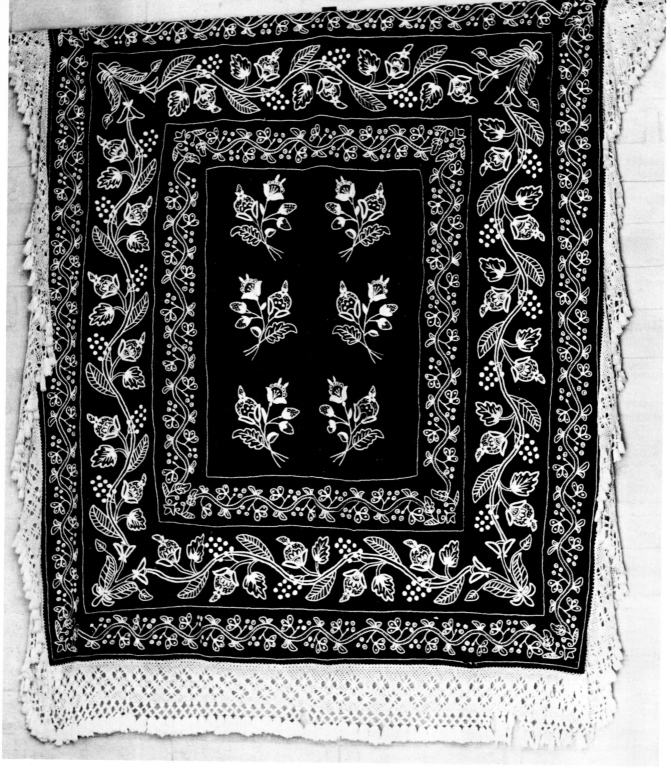

A rich, dark brown cover of finely woven wool carries a hand-embroidered pattern and a crocheted eight inch fringe of woven cotton. The Michoacán village in which it was made, "San Juan de las Colchas" or Saint John of the Bedspreads, is no more, covered now by the lava which flowed from Paricutín. The former inhabitants have gone to other villages and the making of the spreads has become a lost art.

Ralph Gray, artist, and his wife Vicki, live in the small town of Erongarícuaro on the west shore of Lake Pátzcuaro. Here, native women in their homes embroider these whimsical designs which are furnished to them together with the hand-loomed cotton and other materials by and under the supervision of the Grays.

Although the subjects on the guest towels across the top may be unfamiliar, they are, from left to right, as follows: a fish in red, black, yellow and yellow-orange; a cat in white, orange, light and dark brown; a deer in white, apple-green and two shades of brown; another cat, this time in blue, orange, yellow-orange and brown.

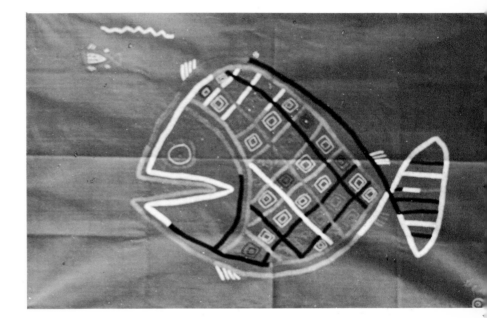

The two pieces on the right are wall hangings, about 30 x 45 inches. The fish is quaintly stitched in white, black and three shades of blue on a mustard-green background scattered with beads.

Below, a bird in white and shades of pink and magenta is being watched by a small but frisky cat in two shades of pink, on a black field.

51

Carápan

Fitted with frosted glass, these shutter-windows provide concealment while filtering adequate natural light. The outline of the glazed opening, although exaggerated, is reminiscent of Moorish screening, seen so often in Mexico.

House of Francisco García Valencia

A quatrefoil window is an architectural detail much beloved by local designers. The name comes from the four foils or spaces which replace the points of the converging circles known as cusps.

Spirited contours of stone crown this opening between *zaguán* and stair hall.
Radiating in the fanlike transom are ornamental bars adapted from old ironwork
found in Toluca, whereas the wrought-iron gates beneath were transplanted from
Puebla.

54

Cancelas, for centuries used as protection and veiling, are frequently found in homes of today. These iron gratings, recently wrought, support a fanciful and much older heading with free standing wheat, leaves and flowers.

Home of José Trinidad Muñuz Rivera

The lower of two knockers on a lofty, metal-sheathed door, 26 feet high, is a handsome example of bronze casting. Round-headed nails forming an over-all diaper pattern, give texture to the background of the heavy circular bosses.

56

the

home

of

Luis Barragan

architect

A Madonna of carved wood
stands on blocks of *sabino*
at the entrance to the *sala*;
a dull reddish-gold figure
against a chalk-white wall.

With his creed of simplicity enriched by contrast of textures and with his strong plastic handling of both space and light, Luis Barragán leads the vanguard of today's architects in glorifying modern principles with the stamp of traditional Mexican forms.

The view looking toward rear garden across the *sala* opposite, is immediately behind the two partitions above. A corner in the shelves holds Santa Catalina of Alexandria.

The four areas shown, one here and the others on preceding pages, originally formed one huge room running from exterior wall to exterior wall. Closely spaced ceiling beams, stained a thin coffee, carry unfinished planks of *pino de Chihuahua* resting on textured walls, 18 feet high, of chalk-white with a pink cast.

Here in the *estancia,* the enduring impress is Luis Barragán's series of steps, seemingly floating upward from gold-piled carpeting to a small mezzanine. No customary pause breaks the rhythm of the flight, nor does the line of an oblique rail disturb nor diminish the strength of a sculptured architectural effect. This stair, made of two inch pine planks, has a freestanding, stepped outline dramatized by painting its underside the white of the walls.

Against the angularity of this room stand the curves of a *butaca,* classic armchair of Mexico, with its frame of *sabino* stretched with cowhide.

A painting by Orozco in browns and greens hangs on the far wall above a low table covered with a hand-woven cloth in deep bougainvillaea. Gathering the colors into a focal point is a low bouquet of soft paper flowers, so characteristically Mexican, in reds, magentas and yellow with sprigs of bright green, arranged in a shallow *batea* on the heavy *sabino* table in the foreground.

Home of Victor M. Villegas

a knowledgeable remodeling

In the restoration of a Guanajuato town house it was only natural that Señor Victor M. Villegas, architect and author of among other publications, "Hierros Coloniales en Toluca," would blend into his own home some outstanding examples of 18th-century Toluca ironwork. Although there had been little done in Toluca of artistic merit in the 17th century, during the next 100 years the crafting of iron blossomed, enhancing a great many façades of that city.

The *barandal* of the *balcón corrido* over the main entrance, opposite, with its wondrously wrought support terminating in a naturalistic lily are handsome representatives of this later period. From one single bar of iron was fashioned this flower ending — the ultimate test of superb craftsmanship of the artist in iron.

0   1   2 ft

62

This railing protects the stairwell of the *azotea* from which there is a memorable view of the city and its surrounding hills. The split and twisted wrought-iron balusters, feathered at their ends, form a novel pattern of S-curves in single-file parade.

From a narrow sidewalk, typical of Guanajuato, these unsymmetrical early 18th-century doors open into their *zaguán*. Pendant motifs with moulded Baroque contours applied on flat raised panels are heavily studded with rows of bossed nail heads.

65

Augustly standing at the central point of this home, San José carries the Christ Child in his arms and, close to his breast, a lily, symbol of purity. Beneath angelic heads at his feet is carved in this single block of stone from the State of Puebla, "Este Señor San José se hizo por Cándido Herandez con la cooperación de los del puebla de Amozoc en 1626."

One end of the colorful library. Applied to the uprights of the bookcase are four richly carved and gilded pilasters from the 18th century, called *estípites*. These, typical of the *Churrigueresque* era, are found in many Mexican churches. The mouldings and rosettes of the long frieze above, painted Indian red, repeat the accents of gold-leaf.

Hanging between Santa Teresa of Avila and Santo Domingo is a fascinating old painting of the Convento Carmelita in the State of Mexico. The escutcheon above, however, that of the city of Guanajuato, has been added.

On this page and facing, are two views of a tortured Christ, carved from *ayaca-huita* against a cross of wrought iron. Above His head, aged beams, grooved and shaped at their ends, are bordered by red and blue wood strips. Painted on the oatmeal-colored ceiling panels between are vague designs of Arabian influence in faded shades of blues, greens, reds and grays.

By great good fortune, one leaf of an original door was found amid the dilapidation of this formerly fine 18th-century home prior to its reconstruction. From it copies were made in a combination of *sabino* and *pino* for the more important openings, including shutters. Their panel designs and method of carving are described by Señor Villegas as *"manierista,"* a fashion between that of the Baroque and the Renaissance.

The *postigo* or "peep" window panel, shown partially open in the leaf on the left, was characteristic of the period.

Topping the high window spreads a *concha* or *capialzado*. The robust scale of its curling outline creates an embracing calm and feeling of protection.

The ceiling brick of the *sala grande*, separated by bands of glazed, yellow brick, are painted with alternating designs in white on backgrounds of tête de négre. One of the most popular articles of furniture in 16th and 17th century Spain and Mexico was the bench, commonly known as the monastery or church bench.

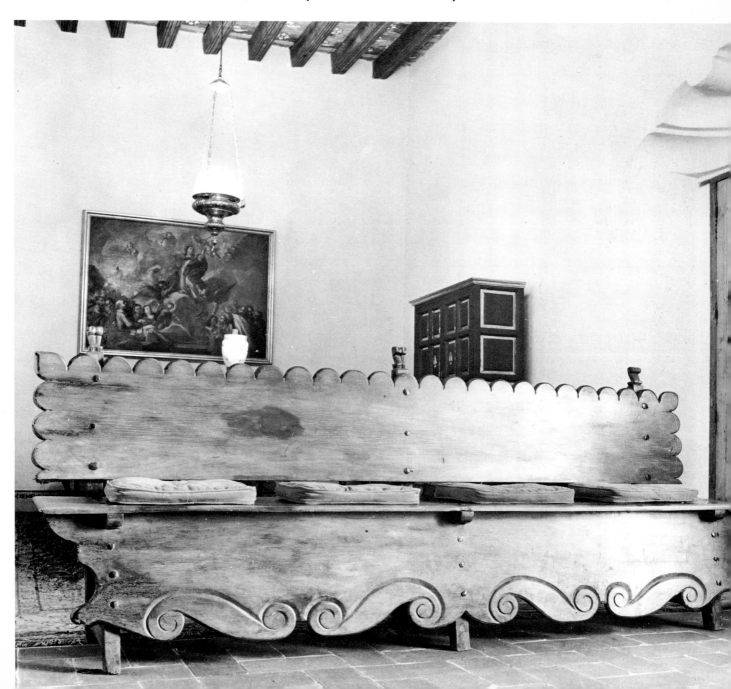

This informal *cancela* in the masonry wall separating outer garden from patio was made by Miguel Covarrubias, the noted painter, and his wife Rosa for their home in Tizapan, an old Aztec village, now a section of Mexico City.

Saint Francis of Assisi, carved from pink *cantera*, stands with humility among lush papyrus in a blue tiled recess. A pink cement shell forms the niche-head and, at pedestal height, three small spouts drip quietly into a shapely basin.

It could happen only in Mexico!
Early one morning, Mr. Mullin
was called to the door by a
neighbor who knew he was an
orchid fancier. She thought that
the man who had stopped at her
house would interest him. Mr.
Mullin got his camera and took
the photograph on the following
page.

The moustachioed Indian had a
rebozo over his head on which
sat a *sombrero* somehow covered
with orchids of the *laelia speci-
osa* family, which he had gath-
ered in the surrounding hills. His
headdress was similar to a Car-
men Miranda creation; for San
Miguel de Allende, beautiful and
exciting.

These same orchids now adorn
the trunks of the jacaranda trees
in the Mullin patio.

74

A spectacular but tranquil tropical garden surrounds a large, glass-tiled pool in Acapulco. Here, on and among the tall coconut palms and graceful almond trees, are 60 varieties of native orchids represented by some 2,000 plants. The many types of crotons add vivid and striking color against the variegated green foliage of philodendrons and countless other plants and bushes.

Overhanging one side of the pool, the thatched roof of the lounge gives charm and atmosphere. The thatching, from the tree palm *palapa,* although shaggy on the exposed side, is neat and orderly on the underside, as shown below. When looking up, one imagines a gentle breeze — thousands of palm-leaf fans.

Photographs by Guillermo Zamora

Club Nautico Mexicano

A power dam, constructed some years ago, has now created an impressive mountain lake six to eight miles long and about 5900 feet above sea level in the Valle del Bravo. Unfortunately, the variations in the lake's level from season to season made the land-based maintenance of anything much larger than a skiff, a difficult matter.

To surmount this problem, a small group of yachtsmen (mostly "Flying Dutchmen" enthusiasts) joined to form the Club Nautico Méxicano. Then, following the ingenious design of architect Jesus García Collantes, the members built, over a period of years, this delightful, little thatched-roofed floating island.

With a part-steel, part-wood frame, the construction rests on blocks of "frigolite," a highly buoyant material, causing it to rise and fall with the lake. Guyed to the steep shore by two chains at 90 degrees it is held off-shore by a rigid foot bridge.

After providing an adequate gangway, the balance of the deck is glassed-in, forming a circular cabin with a brazier under a hanging metal flue in the center. Lockers for gear extend through the wall to form a wide, cushioned settee around the cabin's perimeter. The upper deck, reached by a typical ship's stair, is divided between dressing rooms and card room.

Extended floor beams form slips making for ease in working around a boat while requiring a minimum of dock frontage. A feature is the use of the cantilevered ceiling beams as derrick booms. They, in conjunction with the hand winches on the posts and clever cable rigging, make it possible to lift the hulls clear of the water in a matter of minutes. With fouling reduced to a minimum, there are more hours available for the pleasures of sailing.

Home of Elsa Wagenknecht

A small kidney-shaped pool, gouged out of a steep hillside bordering the Pacific just north of Acapulco, lies below a tropical forest on the right and above an almost sheer drop of between two or three hundred feet to the ocean below on the left. While a practically non-existent late afternoon breeze scarcely moves the water's surface, suspension in the hammock under the thatched roof of the *ramada* makes for complete relaxation.

Home of Mauricio de la Lama
Photograph by Guillermo Zamora

This indoor pool in a glass-walled home, while enjoying maximum sunlight, is protected from unwanted breezes by the Plexiglas strips spanning the roof opening. With the overflow drain running under the open-jointed flagstone flooring of the pool apron, rain is no problem. The unit at the far end, containing the fireplace, TV, record player, radio and small bar separates the pool lounge and *sala*.

Los

Ocho

Caballos

above

Acapulco

Bay

Eight little horses, carved from gray *cantera,* parade along the parapet wall of a garage driveway as the afternoon sun is sinking beyond the entrance to Acapulco Bay. It is said that the name *"los ocho caballos"* was selected for the unusual home shown on the following pages for a very simple reason. During his first visit to México, the owner's Spanish vocabulary included only three words, *"los ocho caballos."*

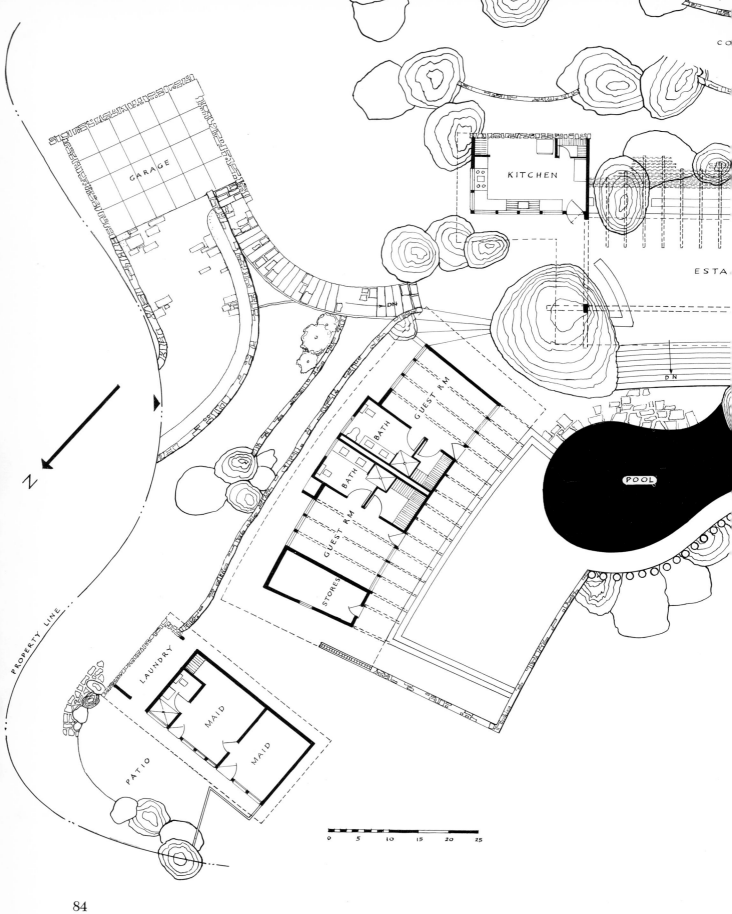

GARAGE

DN

KITCHEN

ESTA

CO

POOL

GUEST RM

BATH

BATH

GUEST RM

GUEST RM

STORES

DN

LAUNDRY

MAID

MAID

PATIO

PROPERTY LINE

N

0 5 10 15 20 25

84

Below, a bridge leads to the masters' suite over a small artificial cascade tumbling down from pool to pool among the boulders: a covered terrace, bedroom and two baths comprise this suite. The baths are unique, troweled river-gravel floors running to the open hillside at the rear are integral with recessed tubs of the same material, highly polished. Countershelves of terrazzo but with beautifully colored, iridescent sea shells were substituted for the customary marble chips.

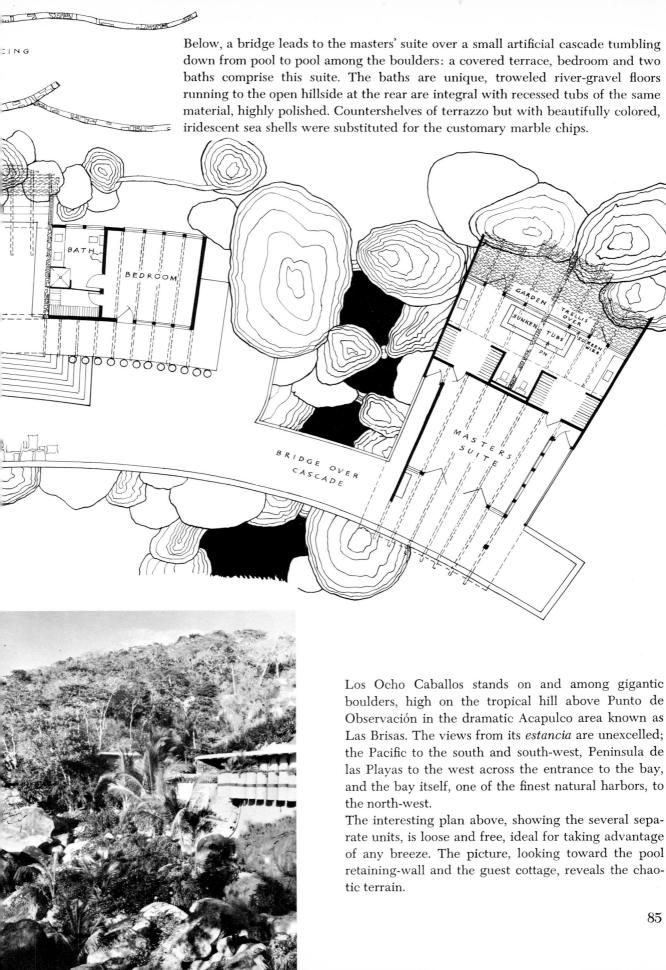

BATH

BEDROOM

GARDEN

TRELLIS OVER

SUNKEN TUBS

SCREEN WIRE

DN

MASTERS SUITE

BRIDGE OVER CASCADE

Los Ocho Caballos stands on and among gigantic boulders, high on the tropical hill above Punto de Observación in the dramatic Acapulco area known as Las Brisas. The views from its *estancia* are unexcelled; the Pacific to the south and south-west, Peninsula de las Playas to the west across the entrance to the bay, and the bay itself, one of the finest natural harbors, to the north-west.

The interesting plan above, showing the several separate units, is loose and free, ideal for taking advantage of any breeze. The picture, looking toward the pool retaining-wall and the guest cottage, reveals the chaotic terrain.

85

The rear wall of the *estancia* is a bit of rocky mountainside overspread with vines and ferns. Just beyond the finished floor, the solid ceiling above is continued to rafter ends with a series of fixed louvers. As well as adding interest, this overhead treatment allows air circulation while, at times, throwing entrancing shadows on the water-worn boulders beneath.

To white cement floor-tiles embedded with chips of marble in gray, white and yellow, and to white ceiling beams carried upon greenish-black beams, color is added in the fabrics. Running along the stone wall is an upholstered seat cushion in golden mustard massed with cushions in chartreuse, purple, turquoise and flaming pink.

Standing at the top of the wide, gently curving flight of steps leading from the *estancia* to the *alberca*, the westerly view reveals, in the far distance, that part of Acapulco which formed, beginning in the 16th century, the port of entry for the rich silks and porcelains which the Viceroys of Mexico received from the East Indies and China.

Protecting the outer edge of the pool apron are concrete cylinders, similar to *pilones*, bonded to the retaining wall. Covered with gray-green stone screenings for texture, they are plugged near their tops, forming oversized flower pots. As may be seen on page 85, this pipe-organ-like regimented effect contributes to the blending of the new construction with the wild jumble of rocks below.

A walk threads its way down from the garage drive between massive boulders to the central unit of this unusual group. Passing the kitchen wing screened by a canvas curtain, one enters the *estancia* at its northerly end opposite that shown on page 86. Here, a masonry bar partially circles another huge boulder. The cushions on the woven reed stools, ranging from blue to green to navy blue recall the colors of the sea lying far below.

Beyond the pool is the guest unit where widely overhanging sage-green rafters carry a built-up white stone roof. Wall panels of soft gray-green stucco are separated by vertical wood posts painted a deeper sage-green. This use of varying shades of green against the greens of the tropical forest beyond produces a delightful sense of coolness.

The kidney-shaped pool lined with small encaustic tile in shades of sea-green and blue-green, receives its decorative jet of water from the spouting mouth of a carved *cantera* feathered serpent which lazes in the sun atop the boulder on the right.

89

This weird and provocative brazier, 28 inches high, is thought by its present owner to be of pre-Columbian origin. A strikingly similar piece of pottery was seen in the small museum of the Instituto Nacional de Antropologia e Historia at Tula where examples of the work of Toltec craftsmen, from 900 to 1150 A.D., are exhibited.

Casa Yara

The Casa Yara is a shop which, while having available many different specimens of Mexican indigenous art, makes a specialty of pottery from Oaxaca and Acatlán. The frog with a gun-metal-like glaze, is black. He would be at home beside a pool and even more content at night, throwing the beam of a candle or electric bulb on some garden path.

Casa Yara

A rather dapper gentleman seems quite pleased to have a cat's or maybe a mountain lion's face in low relief decorating his firebox. When supplied with charcoal, this amusing ceramic stove is quite effective both outdoors or in.

91

Here are three intricate and curlicued ceramic candle holders from Acatlán and Oaxaca. The fourth piece, below on the left, is a modest "Tree of Life," a favorite subject of the former area. Its branches form the heading for an unglazed, white, flower container.

The parochial church of Santa Prisca and San Sebastian, Taxco. Carved stone finials crown the high points of an undulating wall which bounds the west walk to the sacristy. Around the heavily ribbed urn are four handles, each decorated with the face of a cherub while above them rises a symbolic tongue of flame.

93

Photograph by Carlos H. Barba

During the 1770's development began of the vast silver deposits in the rugged hills west of Matehuala. The original town grew to be a city of 30,000 people and was known as Real de Catorce or "Camp of Fourteen" because of the fourteen bandits who at one time over-ran the region. With the playing out of the rich ore, about 1910, Catorce has become a ghost city of 300 to 400 inhabitants.

Above is the main entrance to the Casa de Moneda, or Mint. How puzzling to find in northern Mexico such a knowingly designed Neo-Classic door frame!

Because this architectural trend was not accepted by the Spanish, it was, undoubtedly, the work of some English architect brought out by the mine owners.

The *postigo* head in one of the dramatically handsome entrance doors to the former home of Don Manuel Tomás de la Canal in San Miguel de Allende. A more inspired blending of motifs from the Colonial period would be difficult to find.

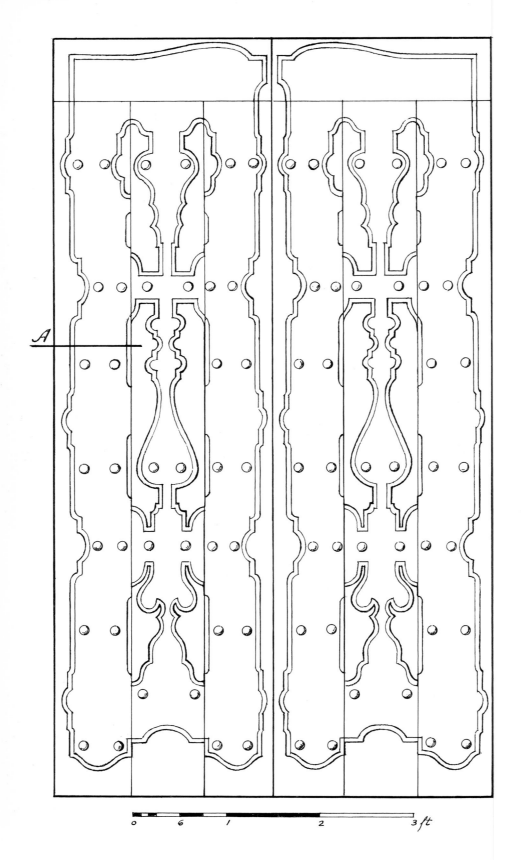

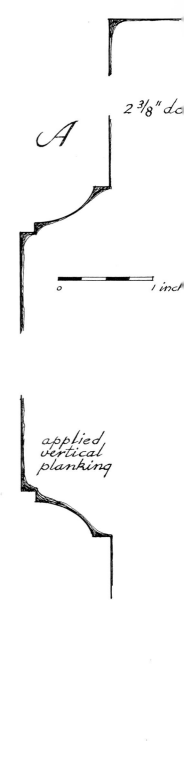

A

2 ³⁄₈ " do

A

0   1 inch

applied
vertical
planking

0   6   1   2   3 ft

96

A recent pair of doors in Taxco whose face planks were shaped prior to assembly, producing these interesting Baroque curves.

Home of Theodore Dreier

Vertical wood rope mouldings and disciplined cast-iron bosses give to these doors an air of stateliness. Both the classic stone frame and doors came from a demolished building in Celaya. They now form the entrance to what was originally the major pottery of Guanajuato, known as San Luisito.

Home of Giorgio Belloli

Home of Hector Alcocer

A door marvelously well suited to the majestic carved stone entrance of which it is now a part, substituting for what must have been one of like distinction.

The taproom at the Posada del Rey boasts a pair of doors with a flair — 3½ inch wood half-rounds intercrossed on vertical planks to make a bold design.

Three doors of widely different character.

At the left, a *cancela*, one of a pair, will perfectly fulfill its dual purpose of ornamental screening or partial concealment and that of allowing circulation of air — of paramount importance in warm climates.

The central pair relies upon small, geometric panels of Moorish heritage for its robust, serene effect.

This type of design with the conventionalized manner of carving in the two upper panels, continued long after the Moorish influence in Spain began to be subordinated to other popular trends.

And lastly, another of a pair. An overall wickerwork pattern, painstakingly carved in a framework of opposing curves of later date and of later European influence.

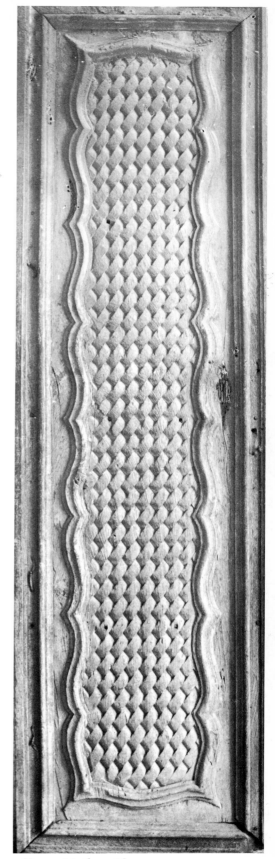

Home of Giorgio Belloli

Home of Anthony Kloman

101

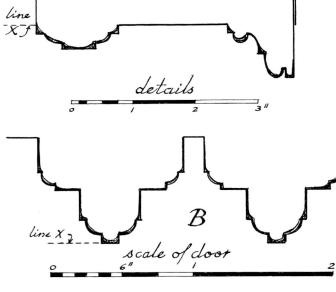

A

B

line
"X"

A

details

0   1   2   3"

line X

B

scale of door

0   6"   1   2'

126

A pair of the entrance doors to Antonio's silver shop in Acapulco are shown here and detailed on the preceding page. The shutter, similar in design, is at an adjacent window opening having a keyblock with an eight inch carved stone pineapple on its soffit.

These closures with their large, open upper panels are ideally suited to a tropical climate. In accordance with Antonio Pineda's imaginative conception, the solid planks forming the lower panels are encrusted with small squares of wood moulding, each of which is slightly out of line with the others and slightly differing in size. The seemingly hand-carved effect together with the turned spindles above, give a decided air of age and richness.

In a region of year-round sun, light and shadow play a leading role in design. Traceries cast by pierced walls and ceilings can prove most intriguing.

Home of Theodore Dreier

The pottery of San Luisito is reborn as a home. In the cool shade of this arcade was thrown some of the finest pottery of old Guanajuato. On the sun-drenched patio beyond, clays were mixed, glazes ground and the earthenware vessels received their initial drying. The present guest house shown on the following pages is in the far background.

Two views of the guest house with its facing of green and pinkish stone. Formerly an adobe structure in which dried earthenware was decorated. A wrought-iron *reja* from Oaxaca, an old *canal* in the form of a canon from Michoacán, and the typically Moorish *tableros* of the entrance door, contribute to the repose and historic niceties of the façade.

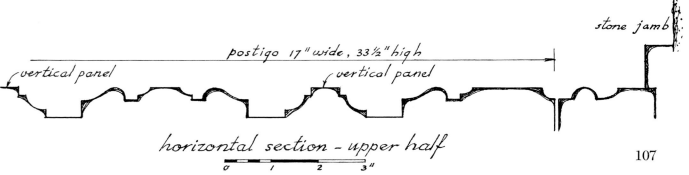

stone jamb

postigo 17" wide, 33½" high

vertical panel   vertical panel

horizontal section - upper half

0   1   2   3"

107

A late door with an open upper panel of turned and twisted wood-spindles fills the arched entrance adjoining the doorway on page 97.

An advantage derived from the use of a heavy masonry wall is the opportunity to have the interior features of a bay window without an exterior projection. The pleasing treatment shown here, with its briskly formed *concha* above a masonry seat, is a part of the *sala*. Of particular interest is the marshaled line of wrought-iron arrows forming the *reja*.

Home of Rosa Covarrubias

The studio of Rosa Covarrubias with colorful mementoes of Mexico and the South Seas enlivening its white walls. On her easel nearing completion, the painting of a Tehuantepec girl in all the finery of a native wedding dress.

Another of Teodora Blanco's highly fanciful figures. With an empty basket, the señora is very likely on her way to market. Her dress, floridly patterned with clay appliqués, brazenly shows the object of her affections — the hard drinking *caballero* on the skirt.

A wall in the Museo de la Ceramica in Tlaquepaque, Jal., carries this entrancing collection of tiny, glazed pottery replicas of jugs, pans and platters in daily use.

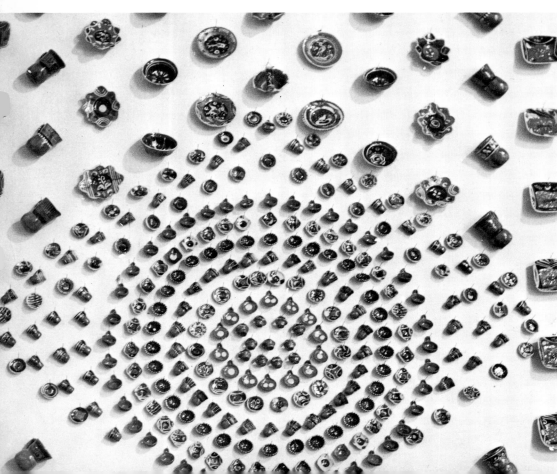

Kitchen dressers, both upper and lower, such familiar articles of kitchen furniture today, were unknown in colonial Mexico. Possibly meeting all needs were a storage closet for basic supplies, and, in the kitchen itself, a projecting shelf or two for wooden utensils, walls on which to hang cooking and table ware, and then recessed shelves for the jugs, pots and pitchers impractical to hang. In doing so the kitchen became a gallery of ceramic art, sometimes primitive, sometimes sophisticated, and always captivating.

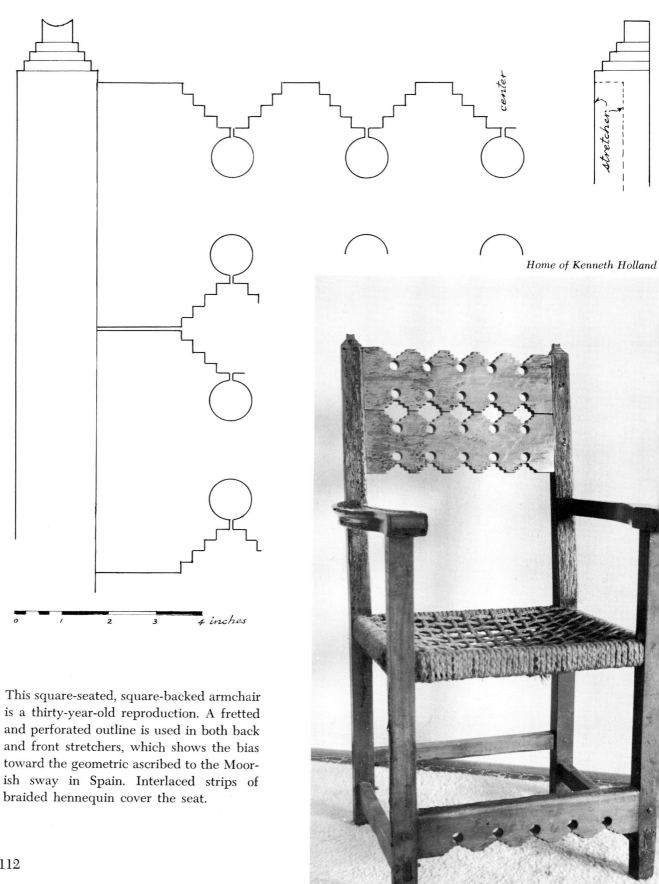

Home of Kenneth Holland

This square-seated, square-backed armchair is a thirty-year-old reproduction. A fretted and perforated outline is used in both back and front stretchers, which shows the bias toward the geometric ascribed to the Moorish sway in Spain. Interlaced strips of braided hennequin cover the seat.

112

From Taxco came this admirably proportioned and balanced chair. Its robust prototype is unmistakably from the mid-16th century Italian Renaissance when four square legs were braced by substantial stretchers. The two in front continued above the seat to become armposts, while those forming the backposts were slightly raked from the seat upwards. Shaped arms frequently terminated in carved whorls.

Home of Rosa Covarrubias

Carápan

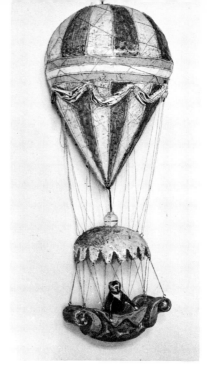

Carved from balsa wood, this blue-uniformed and highly decorated officer from Oaxaca is, for every one of his 25 inches, a fine specimen of a soldier.

In a canopied blue gondola, wired for light, that intrepid English balloonist, the Earl of Oxford, is carried aloft by an enchantingly decorated bag of papier-mâché. Pink and white alternating vertical segments are encircled by a series of white swags under three horizontal bands of green, white and green.

Two Tehuantepec girls with all the furbelows of their native costume stand hand-in-hand forming the headboard of a child's bed. Biege headdresses, blue-gray blouses and yellow skirts (but available in any desired color scheme) with the addition of string, crumpled paper, beads and lace stiffened with glue, then painted, to give a third dimension of low relief.

Atelier of Jeanne Valentine, S.A.

From an old house in San Miguel de Allende flows a most amusing stream of creations, window displays, furniture, toys and so on, things one might find at the end of Alice's rabbit hole. Here the cartoons of the craftsmen on the patio walls, are the work of Nicolas Schlee, son of the owners. He is also the author of much of the inherent whimsey of this atelier's fantastic and delightful output.

115

On this and the facing page are examples of the unique conceptions of their imaginative originators. A little girl in a pale blue skirt carries a typically native, white market umbrella with a light-pink inner lining, to form a table lamp. About 24 inches high.

Atelier of Jeanne Valentine, S.A.

The caricatures of the artisans on another wall of the patio are supplemented by a pair of fighting cocks in heroic scale. Upon dark burgundy backgrounds and with white combs and neck feathers, with blue, green and red tail feathers, white bodies and pincer-like beaks, they are obviously vicious birds.

The bizarre reproduction of the façade of a Peruvian cathedral is in glazed smokey blues and pinks, yellows and oranges.

today's ease

with yesterday's

imprint

This house represents the happy mix of many cultural trends, those from Indian heritage underlying the layer upon layer of customs built up over the years. The techniques of its construction are partly those of the machine, but throughout, the sympathetic hands of the maestros and their craftsmen are evident.

Two of the important lanterns which give a welcome greeting after dark.

The severe gray *cantera* bordering the entrance, whose precedent was that of a Morelia convent, is set in a wall of gray, gray-blue and rust lava rock. Pink *cantera* fragments, somewhat larger than a poker chip, are inserted on the diagonal, like translucent shells, to fill the joints. The omission of these, on the right, was due to a temporary shortage.

The curved line, dominant in the shaping of wood panels during the mid-18th century, has been adopted in this pair of heavy, modern doors.

On the shell-faced console stands an old and weathered statue from Celaya of San Pablo the Apostle, with his beard of many spirals.

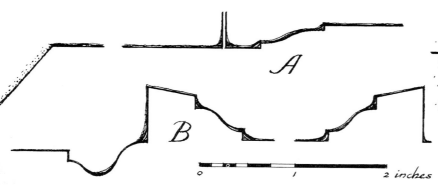

This miscellany of objects adds a festive touch to the formal lines of a Colonial garden façade with its iron *rejas* regimented below a running balcony and with a classic fountain in the foreground.

High on the wall hang two grinning, giant, paper Judases waiting to fulfill their destiny of burning on the streets during Saturday before Easter Sunday.

In a shallow pool lined with yellow tile, stands a fountain of carved brown *cantera*. Its masks, in high relief, look down upon a parade of small, regional pottery ducks. One, a watering-pot from Tzintzuntzan, leads a straggling line of others from Santa Fe and Tonalá.

Looking through the triple-arched wall of the *terraza* toward the fountain shown on page 121. The elegant lantern now resting upon a modified composite capital was originally a church fixture. Wondrously made of tin with delicate openwork bands and with a lacelike high-rising crown, it measures from base to top of finial, 41 inches.

The *cantera* paving blocks have been given a crafted texture with a peening hammer, stressing the accord of homespun tradition with the very newness of this house.

Arabesques, tenderly composed and delicately executed, cover the inner surfaces of a large four-sided dome which rises high above the kitchen and terminates in an ample roof lantern. This ornamental work was inspired by the matchless *Plateresque* façade of La Parroquia in Yuriria, Guanajuato.

½"x 1" lattice

Against a network of shaped cedar strips, unfinished, stand two white horses of the Metepec crafts. Their trappings are outlined in bright yellow, their lips garnet, with cherry-red spots on shoulders and flanks. Despite the extra time involved, Mexican latticework is invariably halved, never lapped.

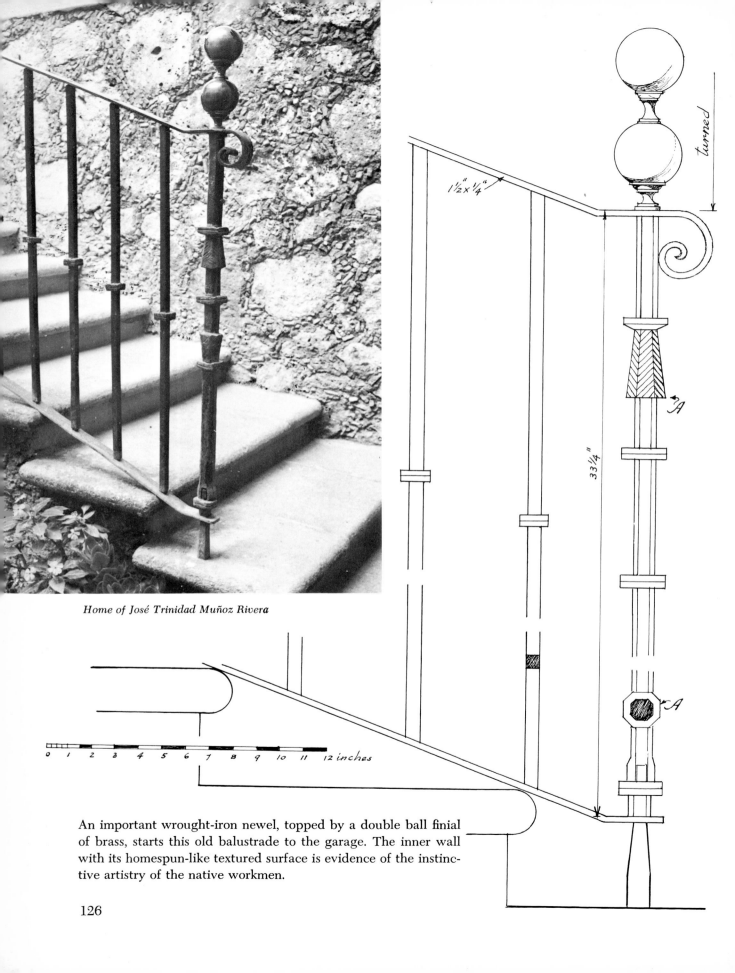

Home of José Trinidad Muñoz Rivera

1½" x ¼"

33¼"

turned

A

A

0 1 2 3 4 5 6 7 8 9 10 11 12 inches

An important wrought-iron newel, topped by a double ball finial of brass, starts this old balustrade to the garage. The inner wall with its homespun-like textured surface is evidence of the instinctive artistry of the native workmen.

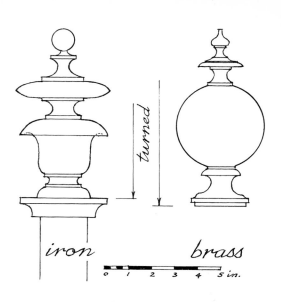

A well-finished brass finial, 8½ inches high, of a snug pineapple design. It has been applied to a shaped iron strap made fast to a wood balcony rail.

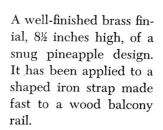

Home of José Trinidad Muñoz Rivera

Home of Anthony Kloman

Home of Dr. Xavier Barbosa

A dainty, flaring crown of brass wire tops a turned newel post of the same metal. Handrail in wood applied on flat iron support; the newel plinth and balusters of iron, the latter ending in cones of brass.

Symbol of hospitality, the pineapple is especially fitting as a stair finial. This is in silver.

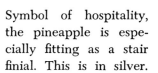

A continuous, hollow, rectangular shape of sheet iron, ½ inch by 1 inch, fairly dances along the street frontage of a new home in Torreón. The two layers of elongated hexagonals, welded together, produce a pattern which is candid and crisp.

Locks come in many different shapes and sizes but one is not often found in the form of a violin. This iron fiddle from Puebla, a copy of an old one, has a hinged finger board. When unlocked, one half of the U-shaped bolt swings free.

Carápan

128

Home in The Pedregal

Through the attenuated hexagonal shapes of flat iron bars and between the masonry of the hooded entrance and the fern-covered mound of lava rock on the right, the open main stairs can be seen, climbing from the under-house carport to the floor above.

129

A panel in a masonry wall, reminiscent of a pre-Columbian temple frieze, but made from ordinary concrete block, provides added ventilation for a garage.

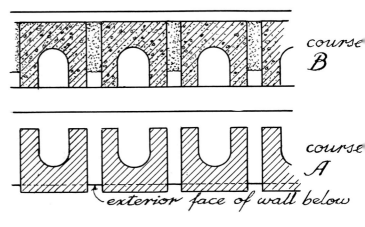

elevation

course *B*

course *A*

exterior face of wall below

Photograph by Guillermo Zamora

Home in Cuernavaca

Hundreds of years before the development of pre-cast masonry units, the *citerilla*, a wall which allowed air passage while giving seclusion, was an important element of design. Here, stock units repeated produce calm and, below, harsh effects.

Home in Hermosillo

Home of Gastón Azcárraga

An overpowering wood gate, 7½ inches thick, is pivoted at the head of a ramplike stairway which leads between high masonry walls of medieval character to a sun-drenched *alberca* below.

In this cleverly devised use of soft-burned brick units, the two exposed corners of each brick, both inside and outside, are rounded. The only mortar used is at the ends of the vertical brick. A most unusual basket-weave likeness.

Home of Hans-Joachim von Block

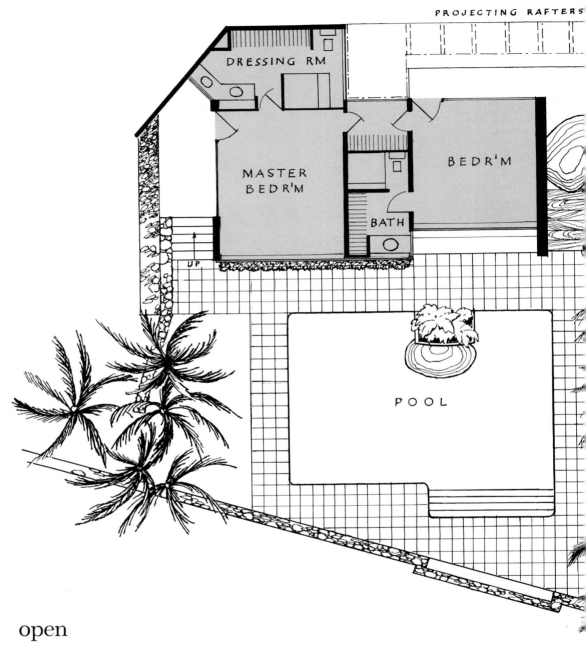

PROJECTING RAFTERS

DRESSING RM

MASTER
BEDR'M

BEDR'M

BATH

UP

POOL

open

to the breezes

over

Bishop's Rock

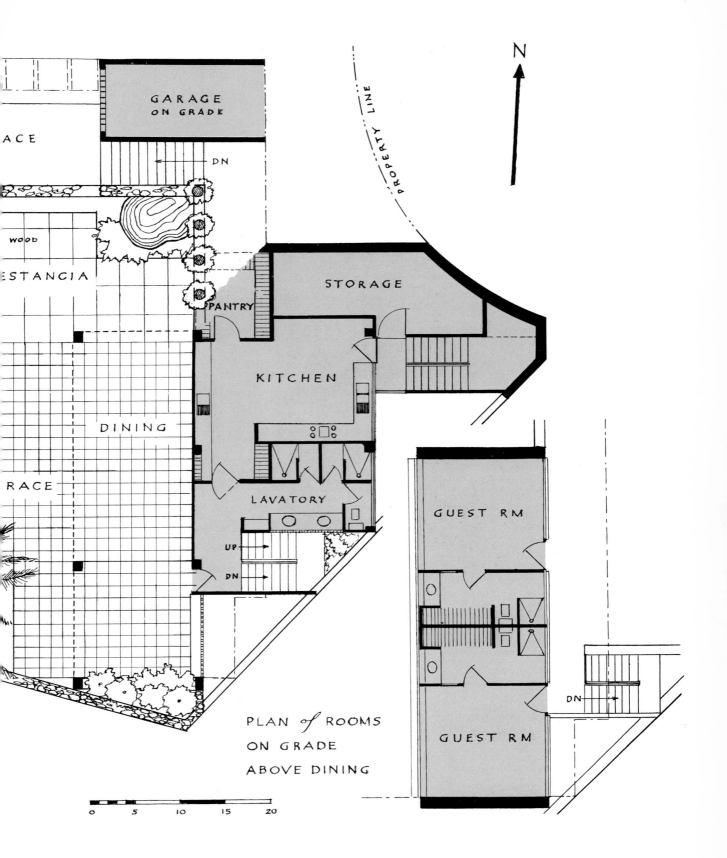

GARAGE
ON GRADE

DN

STORAGE

PANTRY

KITCHEN

WOOD

ESTANCIA

DINING

LAVATORY

RACE

UP

DN

GUEST RM

GUEST RM

DN

PROPERTY LINE

N

PLAN *of* ROOMS
ON GRADE
ABOVE DINING

0   5   10   15   20

Built by its owner, a remarkable home of seemingly colossal scale, whose site on the steep, southerly hillside above Isla Farallon del Obispo, has a commanding eminence.

Below a promenade, guarded by the parapet of the high retaining wall, lies Acapulco Bay, with the harbor entrance and then the open ocean in the background. As a result of knowledgeable planning, the principal living areas are open to receive the benefit of any breeze, but protected by part walls, planting, and the giant roof from all except driving rain storms. Even the four master bedrooms have each two complete walls consisting only of a series of wood-slated jalousies, screened on the inside. When open, maximum ventilation is assured.

In this photograph, one stands near the foot of the main stairway, looking across the *estancia* toward the open entrance court and up to the massive concrete roof some 20 feet above. The rear pierced-tile wall of the garage is on the left and the exterior corner of a bedroom on the right. Four huge flower pots rest on the top of the retaining wall as their philodendron vines cascade to the *estancia* floor below, to mingle with the tropical foliage of a corner planter.

The treatment of color aids the effect of coolness. White walls rise to the white underside of the roof above a floor of white marble squares, finely veined by gray. These whites tend to emphasize the muted colors of the stone masonry, the greens of the planting, the woods of the furniture, and the several colors of the upholstery fabrics.

On descending to the *estancia*, one is suddenly confronted with the view on the preceding page: the Bishop's Rock (Isla Farallon del Obispo) in the foreground, with Peninsula de las Playas and a tip of Isla La Roqueta forming the westerly side of the harbor entrance in the background.

Below: the partially palm-shaded *alberca* parallels the westerly bedroom unit. On the house wall, below the sill line, a variety of white Rose of Sharon, developed in Acapulco, blooms the year around.

A slight turn to the left from the direction of the photograph on page 138 and one is looking over the *estancia* toward the dining area. Above, a bedroom wall which, because of the use of jalousies, can be thrown almost fully open.

Again, looking over the *estancia* with its sunlit patches, but in the direction opposite to that on the facing page. The retaining wall at the rear gives further evidence of the degree to which the house site was carved out of the hillside.

Two proud birds face each other across their egg-filled nest, under a bower of
roses atop this gold-leafed Spanish mirror frame.

A reproduction of a primitive iron cross, 42 inches high, frequently used as a grave marker in the State of Chiapas.

This gigantic and very early chest of twelve drawers was originally one of those used by the priests in the 16th-century Convent of Churubusco. Here, behind the rich, florid carving in high relief of the drawer fronts and their separating pilasters, were kept prized vestments. It is only 44 inches high but 208 inches in length.

Home of Enrique Langenscheidt

Home of Frank Hutchison

Through veneration, street façades in San Miguel de Allende are frozen in the
past. Now and then, when weighty doors are ajar, a vista of the current trend is
seen, but it is somehow not at all unbefitting.

Some ten paces through the stair hall to a wide, tree-bordered terrace overlooking the rear garden — ten paces in distance but two hundred odd years in styling.

Home of Bessie James

The colonial town of San Miguel de Allende lies on the westerly slope of a ridge. Starting below the crest is a grid of narrow streets, both parallel and at right angles with the steep grades. The obvious result is that gardens are, of necessity, terraced. This rear garden climbs up the hill.

Above, the covered, recessed dining terrace is partially bordered by a pair of circular stone stairs leading to the next level. Open tread-ends are protected by pots planted with white, pink and deep pink geraniums. Each line of color terminates on the upper level in a black, three-legged pot containing Mexican *banderas* with their red and white flowers and whose green leaves complete the colors of the national flag.

146

A vined wall with *mirador* above, flanks the recessed dining area on the facing page.

The clay oven, designed by its owner, can be used as a Chinese oven: charcoal in the bottom, while meat, poultry or corn is hung from rods below the dome. The head is a separate unit with holes in its bottom to allow smoke to escape. When turned slightly, any excess smoke pours from its mouth. Practical, as well as a very amusing conversation piece.

147

Home of Frances Stoddard

An invitation to relax. Shaded from the sun by the pan tiled roof, surrounded by potted plants of varied colors against a background of yellow chrysanthemums, and in the distance, the organ-like spires of the pseudo-Gothic parochial church. At left, a gentlemanly creature, sophisticated and soured, condescendingly reviews the approach to a garden stair.

Home of Norman Mac Gregor Jr.

Another haughty and extremely self-satisfied Mexican sphinx, carved from pink *cantera*, rests contentedly among an extravagance of flowering plants.

This *Cruz de Ánimas,* used for family devotions, is a fascinating example of Indian religious art. On the midnight-blue background of an orange cross are painted all the significant symbols of the Crucifixion. The Heavenly Father looks down compassionately as a dove, the Holy Ghost, descends to His slain Son, who was sacrificed to compensate for the original sin of Adam and Eve and their descendants burning in the fires of Purgatory below.

Home of Giorgio Belloli

In a garden south of Monterrey stands a less ingenuous cross, carved from pink *cantera*. It originally was placed near the chapel of an old *hacienda* in the State of México. The entire story of the Crucifixion is sculptured on this cross: the crown of thorns, the nails, the bag of money paid Judas, the rooster which crowed before San Pedro's betrayal, the ladder on which Christ was brought down, together with other details.

Home of Humberto Arellano Garza

Workshop of Giorgio Belloli

Old Indian chapels are a source of delightfully uninhibited motifs, as found on this stone door frame now lying on the ground for assemblage. Little cherubs are suspended between large leaves with a central plumed head of an archangel overlooking a handsome shell.

Examples of the continuing skill of present-day stone cutters is shown below by archangels on the two flanking sections of a keystone.

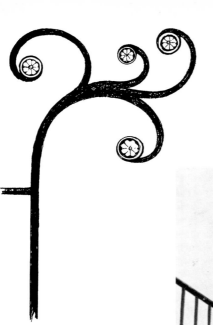

At left, the detail of a balcony support in Guanajuato is remindful of a peacock's cresting.

A recently constructed running balcony with shallow vaults carried upon stone corbels. The simplicity of the *barandal* and the wall ties gives added dignity to this entrance façade.

Home of Anthony Kloman

Superb plaques depicting the four Evangelists with their customary attributes, have of late been added to the rough masonry end-wall of one of the Spanish-Colonial mining *haciendas* at Marfil, so knowingly and sympathetically restored by Giorgio Belloli.

Their great scale, rhythm, color and texture are amazingly akin to the Baroque scrolled pediment looming far overhead. This accord is in part due to the neighborhood origin of these triangles, that of a disused mining chapel in the surrounding hills.

At night, a soft glow of light spreads over each saint from sources concealed under a strong horizontal band course; the effect is dramatic and awesome.

San Mateo stands on the left with a cherub, while recording the human ancestry of Christ.

San Marcos, secretary of San Pedro, wrote his gospel from material given him by his patron, probably the earliest gospel in existence. It is said that, on one of his missionary ventures and while riding out a violent storm near the island-dotted shore of the North Adriatic, an angel told him that a great city would be founded there in his honor. Years later his body was brought back by sailors to this city — Venice. His major attribute, a lion, exemplifying the dignity of Christ, the Lion of Judah, lies beneath his feet.

The third plaque to the right shows San Lucas, patron saint of painters. He stands with one foot on the head of an ox, symbol of sacrifice. And, on the extreme right is San Juan, youngest of the Evangelists. His attributes shown here are the book and an eagle, the latter symbolic of divine inspiration.

154

The use of capitals to distribute loads and embellish column heads comes down to us from ancient times. In Mexico, with the advent of the steel axe and adze, postcaps, or *zapatas*, gave opportunity for the full play of the native artisan's inherent fondness for curves.

On this page, a sophisticated *zapata* and corbel are carved in low relief, while on that following are more primitive examples.

Home of Theodore Dreier

Home of Margaret Gentles & Mr. & Mrs. C. P. Ferring

157

The many massive walls of a former *hacienda* of the 1700's, built to work ore from the seemingly unlimited riches of the famous Valenciana silver mine, fell into disuse over a century ago, due to the change in processing from mercury to cyanide.

Today, some of the walls determine, more or less, the floor arrangements of this house in Marfil. White walls rise simply and serenely, punctuated by functional openings and their knowingly designed surrounds — very Spanish in restraint as well as contemporaneous in repose.

A rust colored lantern held by a black iron bracket gives a fillip to the otherwise all-white façade.

Home of Margaret Gentles & Mr. & Mrs. C. P. Ferring

Guest House of Dr. Xavier Barbosa

A restful, three-sided living terrace, rich with greenery and spiced with pottery from the State of Guerrero, faces a generous, sweeping garden.
An iron candle-holder with delicate tracery swings on the inside wall near the giant philodendron in the corner.

White marble chips give lustre to these pavings. That at left contrasts with a medley of tan and gray pebbles; on the right with those of black.

Home of William Burgess *Home of José Trinidad Muñuz Rivera*

(*Opposite page*) Inspired by the stylized school of concrete fish in the paving at La Parroquia de Lomas de Cuernavaca, the authors schemed this circular walk around a carob tree. The fish, cast in white cement, were laid on a bed of sand, then surrounded by black granite spalls embedded in black cement to simulate flowing water.

Home of Mrs. London Stableford

"A stone *aguador* with depressions in the counter slab for holding water jugs, maybe 100 years old." From this scant information it is tempting to guess the lineage of this highly ornamental piece. Unmistakably, its traits reflect those of the late Italian Renaissance, when everything was subordinated to carving. At that time the human figure in the round was introduced as furniture adornment following the inspiration given woodcarvers by the bronze sculpture of Benvenuto Cellini.

161

A novel home whose austere, masonry street-façade, broken only by the open lobby leading to the recessed front door, gives no hint of the interior nor the enchanting view of the rear garden with which one is greeted upon entering. Great sheets of plate glass, for the most part without mullions, erase any boundries between the rooms and their adjoining garden areas.

Below is a view of the *comedor* with the garden to the right and the *sala* in the distance.

Photographs by Guillermo Zamora

When looking at the house from the rear, it assumes an airy, almost ethereal aspect. Concrete ceiling panels between cantilevered steel beams float out to an almost feather edge over seemingly invisible, sliding and fixed walls of glass. The concept is one of ease and freedom, a true vacation home.

The wide platform immediately outside the *sala* and *comedor* which overlooks the *alberca,* gives an unexcelled lounging area, either with or without shade from the widespreading old tree in the foreground.

Home of Carlos Gomer y Gomez

A sampling of the endless variety of *azulejos*, from the Moorish geometric to later unrestrained patterns. Backgrounds are generally oatmeal in color, with blues predominating in the pattern.

Artes de Mexico Internacionales S.A.

Potters of Tonalá revived a 12th-century French theme in the above central grouping of 9½ inch squares, with earth colors of greens, yellows and deep terra cottas.

In Dolores Hidalgo where the fabrication of handmade *Talavera* tile has continued through the years, the hummingbird, commonly in blue and white, is a favored motif. Here, using rights and lefts, a series of plaques are composed. The legend bordering the plastered masonry hood requests, "Give us each day our daily bread."

Home of Giorgio Belloli

A ventilating hood over the *brasero* and the well-hidden gas stove, slants upward to a flat, curved ceiling in salmon pink brick. Effective tiles in intense blue and white of early Moorish pattern, known as *medio-paño*, contrast with the iridescent hand-glazed surface of those forming the background.

The Mezzanine

These papier-mâché subjects result from applying a fine art to a fine craft medium. "Gemma" Taccagna and her husband, artist Fred Sexton, continue to create these sometimes useful, sometimes amusing and always delightful objects, now widely known and copied.

With white marguerites in relief on a straw-yellow

dress this demure, spit-curled miss holds a rose-colored dove on her folded arms. Busts from the Gay Nineties, 12 inches high, make whimsical waste baskets or flower holders, while the black-and-ivory chess queen, 24 inches high with a sculptured hair-do, is one of a limited edition.

Luxurious bracelets, each signed "Fred Sexton," made of papier-mâché in delectable colors and set with brilliant stones from Austria and Switzerland.

Woven with pliable willow shoots from Tequisquiapan, Querétero, are these three decorative angels with perky braids. The tallest is 32 inches while the tot is 13 inches. From Artes Populares de Tequis.

Home of Mrs. Frank Peters

A fruit-bearing espalier in metal 72 inches high has an allure for delicately embossed metal birds, similar to the one below. The blossoms on the middle branches and that near the top are actually holders for candles which, when lit, throw entrancing shadows on the wall behind.

171

Hojalateria Llamas

Carápan

As fanciful as the ironwork of these chairs are the stories concerning their debut into Mexico. Some claim to be their originators, while others frankly admit to a faithful copying of Paris originals. Whatever the source, they are distinguished additions to a garden terrace.

Shop of Jeanne Valentine, S.A.

Here is a varied collection of silver *milagros* in a primitively painted tin cabinet with repoussé corners and cresting. These votive offerings represent formerly injured parts of humans, such as hearts, heads, arms, legs, eyes, as well as different kinds of animals. They were given to the saints to whom their miraculous cures were attributed.

Home of Rosa Covarrubias

A winsome example of repoussé in light sheet-metal, with its design reminiscent of the Pátzcuaro region, frames a recessed mirror flanked by angled mirrors. It was crafted by Hojalateria Llamas following the design of Jeanne Valentine.

Of rare distinction is this Venetian mirror frame. With restraint, its curved lines hang above a light-colored cabinet, whose many small panels of classic precedent contain carvings related to Moorish forms. Intricately interlaced carvings form the splayed backs of the two chairs, probably traceable to a north Italian model known as "Panchetto." These intriguing side chairs were both designed and carved by their owner, Hans-Joachim von Block.

174

From behind a wide embracing arch, through a glass ceiling, daylight diffuses over bright yellow walls, catching the glossy split leaves of the planted philodendrons. A neo-classic panel painted in grisaille seems to focus the light, giving to it a pronounced third dimension. A splendid carved cabinet of the 17th century blends Spanish-type carving in the manner of the Renaissance.

Shop of Christian Fersen, S.A.

When remodeled for a book shop and display room for fabrics, this former town house went back to the past in order to step into the future. On its smooth, white cement wall the classic pilasters and broken pediment were frescoed in deep gray. At night, a stunning effect of illumination is achieved by means of a series of square lenses, recessed in the soffit of the cornice, through which lamps brighten the entire façade.

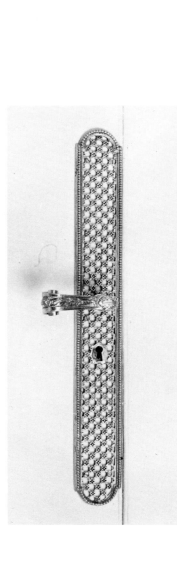

An elegant, pierced back plate and cast-brass lever handle, typically French, are products of Mexico.

And, on a wall of the vestibule, two antique, carved wood cherubs, painted in flesh tones with golden hair and gray wings hold, in festoon, a display of upholstery fabric.

Photograph by Guillermo Zamora

Unmistakably French in spirit
and finesse is this bracket group
of candlesticks. Tôle branches
curve upward from an appliqué
of carved and gilded wood.

Home of Anthony Kloman

Poise and repose are rare accomplishments in decoration. Such an attainment becomes a veritable tour de force when competing with a calm ocean. Arturo Pani shows his expertness in producing "becomingness" between the tranquillity of a vista over the waters of Acapulco and the interiors of his own vacation home.

Colors exchange and repeat from outside to inside: a pale turquoise ceiling over white walls and above a floor of white marble, white slip covers, white leather upholstery. Thrilling is the highly original treatment of the large coffee table with striped canvas mitred skillfully, covering an underframe of wood, then lacquered.

(*Left*) The dining room, seen through an archway, creates an atmosphere of beguiling freshness. Covering the ceiling, tent-fashion, is a printed frabric, ending at the walls in a wave-edged valance. Folds of the same material hang as a backdrop for high-backed chairs in lemon yellow, slip-seated in black horsehair.

A part of the front of Casa Aragón in Acapulco. On the highest
section of Peninsula de las Playas,
the view from the open, rear
elevation toward the mainland
on the north, includes a sweeping panorama of Acapulco Bay,
directly below.

The long expanse of the pierced
wall adds a note of serenity. It
screens the hot afternoon sun
without cutting off the welcome
movement of ocean air.

0 3 6 9 1   2 ft

concrete blocks
16"x 4"x 4"

Casa Aragón

The bayside, awninged upper deck and opening living areas below, all far above the harbor, lend themselves to the ultimate in peace and quiet. A typical gigantic Acapulco boulder seen at the left of the entrance in the preceding view, carries through into the *estancia* above to form a part of the basic construction.

A small shrine to the most beloved of all Mexican saints, La Virgen de Guadalupe.
Assembling various silver alloy castings, sparkling with cut glass stones in the
national colors, white, green and red, this little treasure is unique; probably made
in a penitentiary to while away the time. About actual size.

Through a wide opening, framed by hangings of hand-blocked linen in shades of green, repeated in the connecting valance, a conservatory contributes added size and freshness to a gracious dining room. Small-leafed ivy, forming lozenge patterns on the rear wall, blends with the room's style and tends to dramatize the large, broad-leafed planting in the corners.

In a tree-overhung garden, this small tile-lined pool nestles against the foot of a vine-covered wall. Recessed in the wall, a water nymph, rising from a large shell, fondly holds a dolphin; a piece of early 19th-century sculpture. Copies of this theme have become the signature of the owner, a well-known designer and builder.

Fluted *cantera* columns, each turned from a single piece of stone, carry a convex cornice outlining the exterior dining terrace. The dolphin castings forming the pedestal of the glass-topped table are especially noteworthy in design.

185

The *concha,* ubiquitous in Mexico, here plays two important roles. Over a window, because of its splayed surface of ribs and flutes, it catches and diffuses the entering light. Below, as a niche heading, it decoratively accents a recess, so frequent in masonry walls.

In the early days of the Christian era, it was customary for a pilgrim to carry a shell by which he identified his mission. Saint James the Great Apostle, who later was known as Santiago, the military patron-saint of Spain, is usually pictured in Italian art with a scallop shell and a pilgrim's staff because of the many pilgrimages made to his shrine at Compostella.

The five *conchas* below of delicately wrought silver, resemble, excepting the scallop at the upper right, cockle shells. They range in age from the late 16th to the early 18th century, and were originally used in baptismal ceremonies. The finely formed shell at the lower left with its hinge in the shape of a tight scroll, bears the hallmark which was used only from 1579 to 1637.

Home of Hans-Joachim von Block

An old and very distinguished example of the traditional Mexican over-window treatment.

During the past year, the San Angel Inn, which had been the scene of many historical events prior to 1942 when it began to gradually fall into disuse, has undergone a renascence. The original Hacienda de los Goicochea, built during the early 1700's, later an inn, is once again a well-known restaurant.

The *concha* above is in a wall of the present lounge, one of the few which survived the years without disintegration.

Capriciously trimmed "Tree of Life," over six feet tall (*opposite page*). Actually votive pottery with eight candle holders above the incense pots below carried by women, each supporting, in Acatlán fashion, a duck, a child, a bowl of doves, topped with a rooster. Countless miniature white clay-objects sprout from branches of royal blue.

189

city home of

Arturo Pani, decorator

A wall of white brick espaliered with red-berried bushes, under a roof overhang faced with gray stone, contains a door of brilliant black.

Photograph by Guillermo Zamora

An illusion of space because of one mirrored wall. Upon entering the narrow end of this elegant vestibule, a trick of the eye creates the impression of a square-floored room with the crystal sconce deceptively becoming a chandelier-in-the-round, and the wall, covered with a large-scale Piranesi print, merely a reflection. Black borders a ceiling-center of beige; door black with woodwork beige.

191

In period-piece vein, distinctive and of impeccable taste, using beige, gold and black, with greens to recall the garden tones as seen through the fourth wall of glass. The cabinet-and-portrait composition give a Spanish spice to a room of general European flavor.

Photographs by Guillermo Zamora

Again a mirror, ingeniously placed on the full length of the sofa wall, not only gives an illusive depth to the room but reflects the varying moods and colors of the garden vista. When the latter image is caught, a tapestry-like pattern of greens appears to be suspended in the mirror. Balancing lamp-bases in swirled amber glass were originally balusters, frequently found in local homes of Victorian-tendency under stair and balcony railings.

A magnificent wall niche, carved from wood and heavily gold-leafed, holds young Saint Anthony, favorite disciple of Saint Francis of Assisi. The figure, 29 inches high, of carved wood finished in brilliant, golden *estofado*, lacks a Christ Child sitting on the book, another of his frequently depicted attributes.

A 16th-century Spanish statue, "Virgin holding Child with Bird," stands on a half-moon adorned with cherubs against a mottled wall of "America" stone. Both Mother and Child have glass eyes with enameled faces and hands; their gold-leafed robes, outstanding examples of *estofado* decorated with *cincelado*. Mary's rope sash in red, strikes a subdued note of color, contrasting with the blue lining of her wide sleeves.

The small Christ Child shelters a bird, quite possibly a dove, while resting on his Mother's arm. The halo, flowers and jewelry of the Virgin are detachable. The pearl rosary so delicately held, was added by the present owners.

Above and opposite home of Enrique Langenscheidt

A corner console of the style known in Spain as Philippe V. At that time Queen Anne was reigning in England with vigorous influence upon the trend of furniture lines, especially in Portugal and in Spain, and later in Mexico. In this odd table, a family relationship to the English is clearly seen.

From France, during the 18th century, came sublety and capriciousness to carve a flower basket and turn a curve. This zest has endured, to further enrich the heritage of this land.

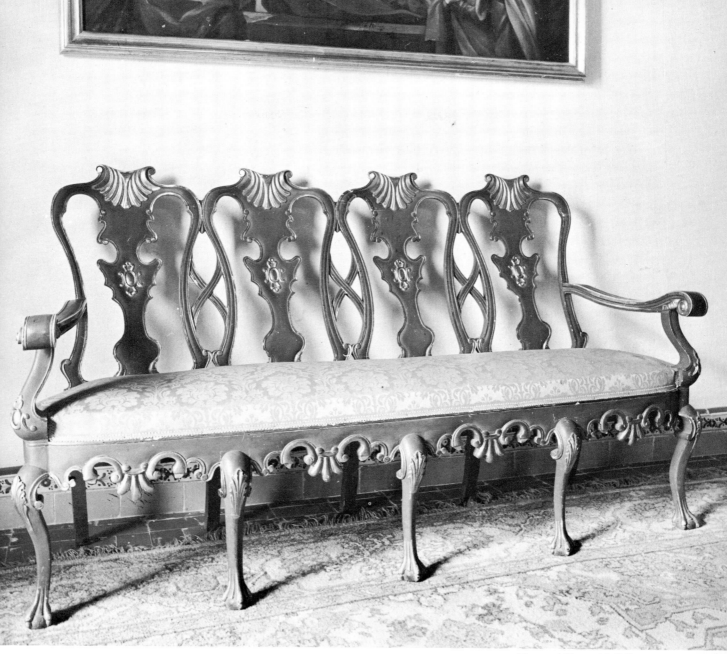

More orthodox in translation of the Queen Anne style in furniture is this quadruple chair-back settee. It is the work of Mexican cabinetmakers who followed earlier Spanish models. Painted Indian-red with ornamental carvings and contour mouldings of splats and arm edges accented with gold-leaf. The seat is upholstered in an old-gold-colored silk damask.

The use of rich coloration, foreign to the originators, was an instinctive liking of the adaptors.

197

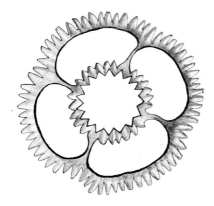

A substantial cabinet of cypress, decorated with an early method of carving, "incised" or "gouged." This was done by cutting away or lowering the ground immediately surrounding each item of the pattern. The figures were then left in silhouette with their flat surfaces flush with the balance of the panel or board. It is quite likely that this and the cabinet in the lower left of the following page were made by artisans from the Pátzcuaro region. Both pieces came from a church in Los Reyes, a town in western Michoacán. As on so much Mexican primitive furniture, the iron rosettes are used for decorative purposes only.

The statue of Santa Ana, mother of the Virgin Mary, is another example of *estofado*. She is depicted here with a book in her right hand, one of her attributes. The white crucifix is considered to be a rare example from Temazcalcingo in the state of Mexico. Quite oriental in conception, it could well be the interpretation by some Indian craftsman of a Philippine ivory crucifix which had come to Mexico during the 17th century.

198

Wood ceremonial mask of the Mayo Indians, a tribe living in the Navojoa district of Sonora, blood brothers of the Yaquis. The tan face is framed by a seemingly close-fitting "super-man" head-covering, colored dark brown with incised white lines. The hairs of the white beard are slightly longer than the 7-inch face.

Below, a small cypress cabinet, only 39 inches high to the flat top, has its door panels ornamented with the most delightful little angel faces alternating with flower like rosettes, all carved in relief.

At lower right, a flamboyant cabinet of reds, gold and mirrors. The top is painted red, then antiqued and varnished while all mouldings are gilded over bole. On the mulberry-colored flat panel at each door, mouldings outline mirrors to which carved-wood, gilded motifs are applied. The ends, 20 inches wide, are treated in a similar fashion to the front which measures 45 inches wide by 43 inches high.

Home of Lena Gordon

Home of Humberto Arellano Garza

Home of Anthony Kloman

Because of the cures attributed to the hand-carved Guadalupe on the central panels, the doors of the old cupboard are practically covered with *milagros* similar to those on page 173. It was used to store Holy Vessels in a sacristy near the altar. The 17th century figure of Christ over the cupboard was modeled from ground corncobs and then painted.

An old silver Porta Paz, repoussé in high relief on a wood backing. The Greek Cross as the central motif radiates beams on a speckled field, surrounded by intricately tooled curves.

Pair of turned, silver candlesticks bearing a hallmark which was in use during the first half of the 17th century. Standing 11 inches high, they are delicately chased in classic patterns.

divided between
past and present
by a wall

Due to San Miguel de Allende convention, the original street walls of these two houses are unchanged, merely refurbished, while the construction behind is entirely new. The following interiors are those of the house at the right.

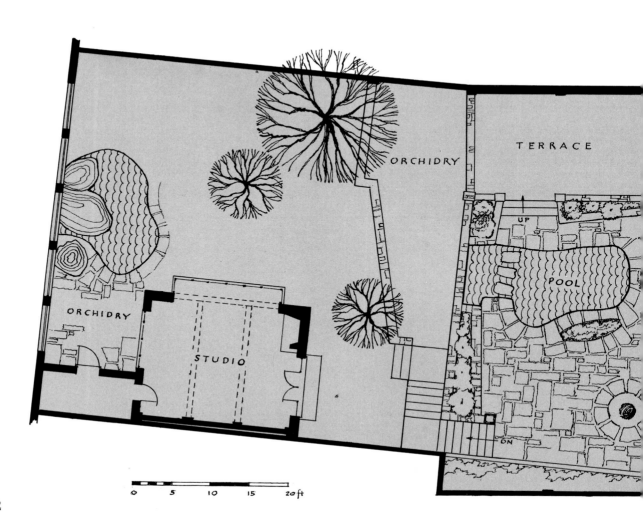

ORCHIDRY

TERRACE

ORCHIDRY

UP

POOL

STUDIO

DN

```
0    5    10    15    20 ft
```

Looking back, when passing the *sala*, to the arched wall on the next page surmounted by the lacelike screening on page 209.

Home of Norman Mac Gregor Jr.

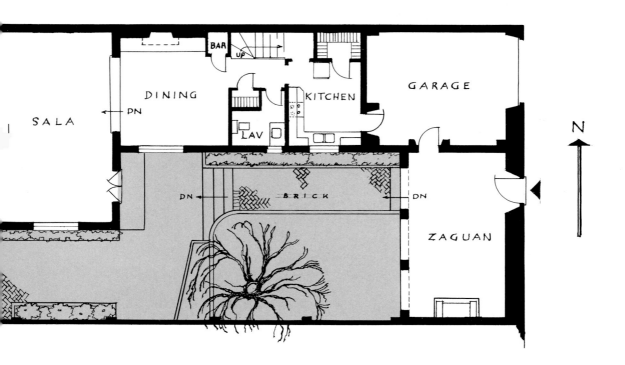

An unexpected transformation takes place on passing from the cobbled street directly into this fresh white-walled room, with its old-wood beamed ceiling and brick floor. Three solid walls, the fourth a series of arched openings, one of which is shown on the left overlooking the garden approach. The furniture and lamps in iron were designed by James D. Ely and manufactured in his shop. Some of the chairs are painted black with black-and-white-striped cushions; others have been given a verdigris finish with yellow cushions, while the wall seat, whose back hangs from lion door knockers, is upholstered with a tweed fabric: black, gray, white and yellow. Above, on the wall immediately behind the entrance door, slotted metal strips with adjustable brackets carry a writing counter and a series of book shelves.

Here and following are two views of the *sala*, a handsome, high-ceilinged room with one wall of chinked rubble masonry acting as a foil for the sophistication of the appointments. The doors above open on the terraced garden to the west, its pools, flowering plants, great trees and shaded areas for orchid culture.

The furniture here was the work of the owner, an architect and professional designer. The wood used is known as "*caoba*," a kind of mahogany; the stools and chairs a rich brown, while the long coffee table is a brilliant black, heavily lacquered. The upholstery colors range from the white Naugahyde of the stools to the Empire-green of the armchairs, to the deep biege of the sofa with its red and gold cushions.

Up two risers from the *sala,* looking across the *comedor* toward the bar and stairs to the floor above: a chastely formed fire-hood, painted off-white, carries the initials of the Virgin Mary in silver, partially surrounded by alternating rays of silver and pale green. The hood's base is decorated with a row of cast bosses finished with verdigris.

Home of Norman Mac Gregor Jr.

A several-patterned screening of burned clay formed with one cleverly designed
unit, gives a degree of privacy to the open sun-deck.

209

At the left, the originally turned spindles of doors and fixed panels have been replaced.

Lovely, gay *cancelas* of the past century are highly appreciated by searchers for the old and decorative. Walking by the open entrances of Morelia's town houses, glimpses through the *zaguans* usually reveal these turned and intricately jig-sawn screens.

What a pleasure for the artisan who with saw, jig and lathe produced these doors, with side panels and the circular-headed transom topping it all.

Villa Montaña

A distinctive room of scale, with stonework and wood ceiling typical of the Morelia
area. In the foreground, the *estancia*, the *recámara* on the rear raised level and,
detailed opposite, the tightly coiled wood stair tucked into the corner.

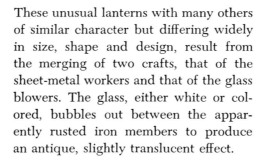

These unusual lanterns with many others of similar character but differing widely in size, shape and design, result from the merging of two crafts, that of the sheet-metal workers and that of the glass blowers. The glass, either white or colored, bubbles out between the apparently rusted iron members to produce an antique, slightly translucent effect.

A mid-18th-century *sala*, a result of the vast riches which flowed from the Valenciana silver mine, high in the mountains above Guanajuato. Built by the Conde de Rul, this much-pictured house typifies Spanish characteristics of those years — dignity, vigor and concentration of interest. Were this room, after two centuries, stripped to its plaster skin, would it not, due to simplicity and high-ceilinged proportions, strength and composure, be a likely setting for today's incoming trend?

High in key — white painted walls of hard-burned brick contrast with the salmon pink of the soft, flat brick between old ceiling beams of yellowish brown, and with those on the sweep of the stair soffit. Inspired by the pagodas of Thailand, an enormous birdcage sparkles with highlights.

216

The eye follows the steppings of the slab treads and of their ends protruding through the rectangular slots of the latticed wall. Green carpeting completely covers platforms and treads, nicely contrasting with the nut-brown of the wood.

James Norman writes, "The people are inveterate bird fanciers, and have been since ancient times. Bird-cage building, thus, has become an important facet of the architectural arts of Mexico." This four-story dwelling in brass, over five feet high, was designed by Monte Hart.

Galería "Trini"

Edificio "Cremi"

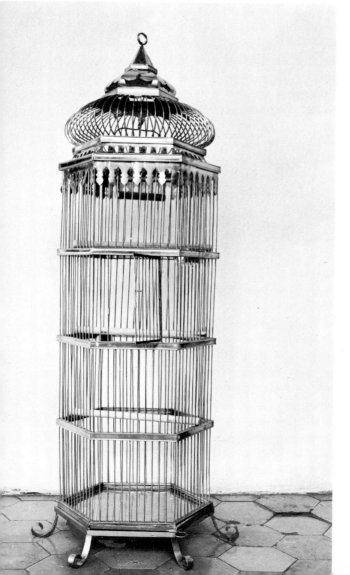

Sala de Artes

One of the several types of typical 17th century Spanish headboards, actually Portuguese in origin. Produced by Artes de Mexico International S. A. in stained pine with turned posts, rows of delicately turned balusters, carved horizontal members, the whole topped by a crested trinity.

Found in a demolition yard of Mexico, D. F., this former wrought-iron garden railing now serves with a distinctly Spanish flavor, as a side- and head-board.

218

Home of Francisco García Valencia

Thea Ramsey and Elsa Wachter, decorators

The presidential suite of the Acapulco Hilton boasts this dreamlike headboard, jig-sawn from plywood and offset from the wall. Inspired by traditional china paper cut-outs used in rural fiestas — one of the most endearing of the popular minor arts.

Home of Dorothy Macdonald

"In Colonial times the color combinations for *talavera* decorations were usually white, blue and yellow. Over the centuries the delicate precision of the Spanish craftsmen has given way to Indian touches.... Orange, black and green have been added...." James Norman

Ceramics and dinnerware of a new sort by Felix Tissot of Taxco. Painted by natives of the neighboring hills in patterns entirely of their choosing. Backgrounds of faint blue with rabbits, hummingbirds and what-nots in buffs and blues.

On a shelf supported by a carved, gold-leafed bracket with mirrored quatrefoil as central motif, stands the Infant Jesus. His face, hands and feet are enameled, while His gown is in *estofado* with a minute floral pattern on red, then gold background.

222

An Indian conception, 22 inches in height, of Mary Magdalene, prior to her conversion, has an enameled face in flesh tones and articulated arms of cloth. Here again, the oversized hands are characteristic, and here again, her skirt in red and gold is another beguiling instance of *estofado*. Her blouse with embroidered flowers and Maltese cross was made by Louise Belloli. Extravagant eardrops were added to her pierced ears and a doll's wig was substituted for the lost original.

Home of Giorgio Belloli

At the left (*opposite page*) are two saints, San Isidro and San Juan the Apostle, each showing the inclination of the native sculptors of that time to exaggerate the proportions of heads, hands and feet.

San Isidro, with halo of gold-leaf and gilded pants rolled high as he drives his diminutive black oxen. It is said that his farming activities were taken over by an angel from time to time so that he could attend holy services.

The flowing robe of San Juan is a well preserved example of *estofado*, its decoration beautifully executed. As is customary in Mexico, his attributes are a black lamb on a book which he carries in his left hand.

After

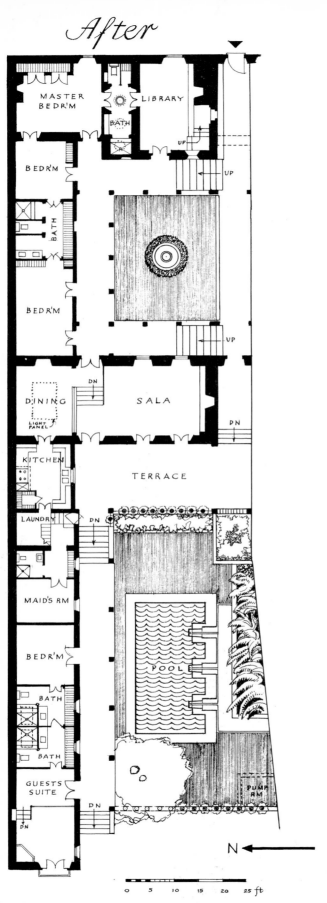

MASTER BEDR'M
LIBRARY
BATH
UP
BEDR'M
UP
BATH
BEDR'M
UP
DN
DINING
SALA
LIGHT PANEL
DN
KITCHEN
TERRACE
LAUNDRY
DN
MAID'S RM
POOL
BEDR'M
BATH
BATH
GUESTS SUITE
DN
DN
PUMP RM

N

0   5   10   15   20   25 ft

224

Before

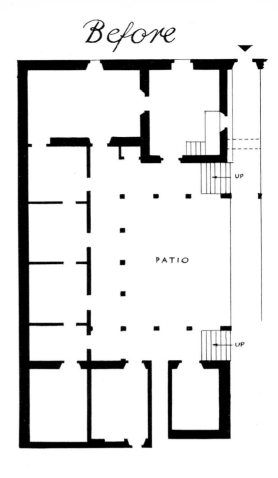

UP
PATIO
UP

a sow's ear

becomes

a silk purse

On a street immediately west of San Miguel de Allende's *Monjas* de la Concepción, a front wall hid a series of rooms ranged around a patio crowded with the chickens and pigs of the several families jammed into these confined quarters. A comparison of the two plans clearly shows the transformation which has taken place.

Home of Elton Hyder Jr.

This street front retains its original identity, re-stuccoed and then painted a mauve above a warm, dark charcoal dado.

After entering, the former lowered walk passes the old patio (now with a fountain in its center and with walls of a deep Mexican pink), and leads to the welcoming figure of San Miguel. Here, to the right, a covered *terraza* has a pleasing view over the *alberca* and on to the low rolling hills westward.

225

Part of the wall separating the *terraza* and *sala*. The old roof plate remains as an amusing saw-toothed belt course of one-inch brick. Delightfully free, frescoed swirls over the French windows revive a charming Colonial fashion. A bowl of large paper poppies in reds and pinkish whites rests upon a cast-cement shelf over a handsome grille. Again, the wall color is Mexican pink, with bands around the windows of soft mulberry, then a bluish gray, while the frescoes are in bluish grays tinted with pink.

Looking through the terrace railing with its leaded ornaments and its integral flower-pot holders, toward the high-ceilinged *corredor* of the new wing on the right.

Here one becomes more intimately acquainted with the carved-stone functional item known in Mexico as a *canal*, more universally, as a gargoyle. While a circulating system is the main water supply, these three horses, removed from their normal duty of serving a roof on a rainy day, now dribble additional water into the pool.

228

From the intermediate level of the rear garden, across the *alberca* toward the covered *terraza* and to the lanterned dome of the *Monjas* de la Concepción.

On the left, the arresting end-wall of the *sala* with its split-random stonework.

Inherent to Mexico by way of Spain, indelibly impressed by the Moors, came a stressing of ornament around an essential feature. Following this tradition, a gold-leafed, carved wood over-piece crowns the fireplace with the monogram of the Virgin Mary. Above, these same initials, M A, are embroidered, over padding, with small white beads and sequins of brass on a silk background of a faded cherry color. About 16 by 20 inches.

On the fireplace wall of the small library are wood panels, originally part of a Oaxaca altar. They were carved in low relief by Chiapas craftsmen in the latter's interpretation of the *Plateresque* and provide a setting of grace and calm for the large figure of the Madonna, which was separately applied.

231

A wood column, encircled by a carved leaf-motif, carries a heavy wood lintel under the pierced clay-tile panel which gives light and ventilation to the bathroom below.

The carved stone lavatory with pedestal in the master's bath, was formerly a baptismal font. It now has an enameled lining, with brass barn swallows dominating the water controls.

Home of Hans-Joachim von Block

Home of Elton Hyder Jr.

A small and old Spanish angel, 26 inches high, dances on a green globe. His flesh tones blend with the pink of the niche, his wings are golden and his scarf is an olive green.

Rising from the lower level to the very high ceiling of the inviting guest-suite, is a long and thin chimney hood, giving to this space an elfinesque look. The basin of a 16th century-Oaxaca fountain was cut in halves to provide the lintel and the base of the raised hearth.

Alongside rests an armchair, restrained in line but unbelievable in its over-wealth of "gouge" carved decoration, an extravaganza of 17th century in Spain. And, above the few steps leading to the lowered area, an unidentified wood figure with haunting glass eyes and an appealing gesture, stands on the elaborately carved, gold-leafed bracket.

Home of Mauricio Weissman

An entrance with rhythm and dignity is highlighted by the small, recessed fountain on an otherwise blank wall. The massing of white azaleas softens the formality of the carved, white stonework.

The water nymph on page 184 reappears; this time at the deep end of a tile-lined pool with a mosaic bottom, in a balustraded garden.

An engaging basket, 26 inches high, is made from the willows of Tequisquiapan. This austere cat, with elegant bow tie and long curled tail, is equally at home serving as a two-bottle hamper or when carrying damp beach clothes.

The *alberca* below is actually a part of the house, protected on one side by heavy planting, on two sides by high walls, and on the fourth by the house, into which an arm of the water projects. This channel at the far end to the right passes under a sliding glass door and terminates in the enclosed pool lounge on the following page. Here, on cool days, one can warm oneself at the large vented brazier in the center of the room, swim out under the door, and return without body exposure to the outside air. The view shown is a part of the surprise which awaits at the foot of the forbidding stairway on page 132.

Home of Gastón Azcárraga

Artes Populares de Tequis

(*Opposite*) Delightful in sumptuous simplicity cast screening curves with the garden wall. Of two planes held apart by shaped separators and offset, it gives variety to patterns and shadows.

Home of Gastón Azcárraga

A formal *sala* opens from the high-ceilinged *estancia* and leads to the *comedor* on the page opposite. In a wall of white marble veined with gray, the fire-box is treated in a novel manner; instead of being a dark pocket, this opening, with its back of glass, acts as another window. Other walls are covered with an Empire-patterned fabric of greenish white above a carpet in near-white. The green of twin upholstered stools in the foreground recalls in deeper tones the muted green-gold rosettes of the walls. Browns, golds and yellows, French blues and beige weave an adept scheme of colors.

Looking from the dressing-room wall of the pool lounge, past the brazier to the entering arm of water just inside the outer glass wall. Beyond, a *zonpantli*, a native Indian tree whose red blooms when boiled, taste, it is said, like mushrooms.

Home of Gastón Azcárraga

Home of Dorothy Macdonald

A rare, primitive *santo* with a removable straw *sombrero*. The carving of his robes is gessoed, then painted in flat, earth colors —coral, pale blue, gray, and gold-leafed. Bought from the nuns of a convent in Temascalcingo, a village south of Toluca, his identity is uncertain, but, because of the book, he was undoubtedly a saint revered for his teaching.

(*Opposite*) Once a year the little village of Tecomatepec, one of the pottery centers with the strongest Indian tradition, empties itself into Taxco for "the Day of the Pitchers." These pitchers or little jugs are bought in great numbers and exchanged among friends, a sort of Mexican Valentine's Day. Their burros are also loaded with figurines in shades and glazes of yellow: deer, horses, goats, some in bizarre polka dots.

These two horses with riders, six modeled in almost precisely the same manner, with the same straight, tapering legs as two now in the Museum at Olympia, shown in "Greece in Color." They are described as "small clay figures (sub-geometrical if not 6th century B. C.)."

Galería "Trini"

Photograph by Armando Salas Portugal   *Home of Roberto Berdecio*

One of the more striking of contemporary homes, although built in 1950 when *Jardines del Pedregal* was still in its infancy. Only a limited idea of the barren, lava-strewn terrain, now verdant with plants and trees, is given by these pictures.

Photographs by Max L. Cetto

Above and below are views of the wide entrance court, while opposite, glass of the large *sala* window reflects a garden stairway, chiseled from the rock, and the distant mountains. Plain wall surfaces, knowingly punctuated here and there by openings constantly reflect the play of changing light.

In old Mexico City, home of the bracket sketched below, and in Guanajuato, that of the support above, such awnings seem to have all but disappeared, leaving their hardware behind. A noticeable exception, however, is their use on shops, hotels and the like where graceful lines and cooling shade lures the passer-by.

The two awnings on these pages show the continuing appreciation in Puebla of stylish sun-shades. The roll-up, roll-down curtain may take its cue from the Victorian, but nonetheless — a sensible solution.

plastic   *cloth*   *metal*

cloth   metal

After a period when many of the larger urban homes had their eyes staring street-ward, they now, and happily, have reverted to the Moorish manner of "looking inward," their privacy maintained by high, property-line walls. Entrance gates for automobiles and foot passage vary considerably in design; in many instances they are roofed, affording protection from the summer rains.

On the preceding page, the upper picture shows a steel wall, its white panels and black trim painted similarly to those of the main house in the background. Below, a masonry wall of dark gray basalt laid random irregular with fairly tight mortar joints, has large planters of a lighter colored flagging on each side of the entrance. The gates, constructed with hollow-steel vertical members, 1¼ inches x 6½ inches, give a feeling of security commensurate with that of the wall.

Above, an example of a majestic wall-entrance with a roof pierced to let in the sun and permit high planting at an inner corner. The doors are wood, vertically sheathed. The lintel and right-hand wall faced with large beige-gray stone slabs, are offset by the horizontal, beige-pink stone of the opposite jamb.

Home of Dr. Xavier Barbosa

From a narrow, sloping street, through a walled opening and you are in this story-book courtyard with the lush greenery of a terraced garden beyond the octagonal-based stone fountain. Stairs from the open vestibule lead to second floor bedrooms, while the door to the right opens into the *sala*. Here, the fantasy basket on page 127 tops the main newel post.

A detail of the laughing lion, carved from pink *cantera*, as he sits above an old, weathered console at the corner of the three wide entrance steps.

248   A study in angular light and shadows with a touch of Luis Barragán in the flight of cantilevered steps.

One of a series of windows, the work of sculptor Mathias Goeritz, in the cupola of the Iglesia de San Lorenzo, shows in dramatic outline the great keys of San Pedro.

And with them, the book is closed.

Shipway, Verna (Cook), 1890-.
   Mexican homes of today.